BENEATH
THE SURFACE

Uncovering the Treasure in Old Wounds

Mary McGrath

To Carole
With lots of love
Be happiness
Mary McGrath

BALBOA
PRESS

A DIVISION OF HAY HOUSE

Excerpt from THE NEW JERUSALEM BIBLE, copyright (c) 1985 by Darton, Longman & Todd, Ltd. and Doubleday, a division of Random House/Penguin, Inc. Reprinted by Permission.

Balboa Press books may be ordered through booksellers or by contacting:

Balboa Press
A Division of Hay House
1663 Liberty Drive
Bloomington, IN 47403
www.balboapress.com
1 (877) 407-4847

Print information available on the last page.

ISBN: 978-1-9822-2065-5 (sc)
ISBN: 978-1-9822-2066-2 (e)

Balboa Press rev. date: 01/23/2019

CONTENTS

PREFACE

The initial inspiration for this work came during a weekend retreat led by mystic Andrew Harvey. He has an intense passion and personal grief about environmental issues. In his words and presence, I sensed a wound—not a wound peculiar to him but a common wound in the human psyche that generates great pain, preventing us from feeling at home, healthy, and joyful in our world.

I prayerfully asked for help from the universe to gain some insight into the source of that wound, which was creating our frenetic dance with the annihilation of life as we know it on this planet. Once I had asked the question, many sources emerged from both within me and around me, pointing at previously unnoted connections. The masculine–feminine split in the human brain seemed to appear at the center of the inquiry. Our two most basic instincts—one for dominance and one for nurture—appear to be at odds with each other in arenas most vital to our survival.

With this in mind, I attempted to source this book using both sides of my mind—the intuitive and the rational—giving both equal honor. This was not only a difficult way to write but also a difficult way to read. Writing and reading are linear processes. The soul and growth move in nonlinear ways. I ask for the reader's patience and indulgence. Using deep intuition and listening to the energy in my being and in the writing of many explorers of the human experience has led me to some intriguing explanations of evolutionary wounds. We can heal these wounds if we can acknowledge them. I pray that you will find the challenge of trying to stay present, and listening with both body and mind, reason and intuition, as rewarding as I have. But I warn you; it can disorient you. That reaction itself lies at the center of the wound.

In this preface, I share some experiences that shaped my particular questions in hopes that you will be more inclined to patiently accompany me through the shifting progress of this book. I have been shaped by two formative personal experiences, which I feel I must share if anyone is to understand my thinking in regard to boundaries. Both experiences threatened my edges and limits. Both demanded a reintegration of my identity as a human. My consciously chosen goal in the way I processed these impositions was to avoid transcendence as an escape from the complexity. Instead, I chose to be lovingly present with real gratitude and awe to my species' evolutionary choices in defining our shared reality, with all its limits, as I integrated these experiences.

My first career was in education and early childhood development. Growing attuned to the ways human perception grows and the ways humans think and feel was the gift of that experience. I lived my personal life on a few acres on a mountainside in Vermont, raising a small flock of sheep and gardening. The first formative imposition happened on a spring day in my late twenties. Moving between house and garden, I passed the flat stump of a large spruce tree that had been cut several years before to build our cabin. I appreciated this particular familiar stump; I frequently used it as a table for tools or my tea mug as I moved about. On this day, the stump transformed. It appeared as shimmering, vibrating energy. The stump was the only object in my visual field that appeared transformed. I perceived the stump as vibrating specks of light amid much empty space, and I had an urge to reach out and put my hand inside the decaying wood. But my rational mind did not fully trust the moment, and I refrained with some vague fear that I might not be able to reclaim my hand. The stump transformation lasted only a few moments.

Afterward, I kept the experience a secret. The fact the tree stump was the only object transformed in my field of vision eliminated the possibility of a migraine having caused it. With no drug usage to explain it away, for years, my rational mind watched for some repetition that would indicate a brain malfunction. But beneath my doubts and fears, at my core, I felt that I had witnessed reality. And I responded to my shimmering stump experience by re-enrolling at the University of Vermont to study physics, seeking to somehow grasp the energy that I had seen in the stump. My study confirmed my momentary perception of matter as vibrating energy and light. In turning to science, I did not deny the spiritual or any other aspect of the experience. To me contemplating light, time, and energy was contemplating God. Physics was a spiritual pursuit. No boundary existed between the scientific and the spiritual. At the speed of light, there is only one moment. Nothing is lost. The energy patterns of matter transform and recreate new form.

For me, the study of physics created a profound trust in the universe. I recognized that the light that is within all matter, the light that is the essence of all matter, is divine. I began to attend to the mystery within form with a new, open-eyed view. This did not displace a God of love, the basis of my old spiritual structure, from the center of my cosmos. Quite the contrary; studying physics slowly but surely helped move me from looking for God in transcendence to seeking the divine in immanence, in matter, in my body, and in the dynamics of the cosmos. Not expecting answers to my questions only led me to more insightful questions; it freed me to be present to my world and my perceptions with less judgment and more playfulness and, most consequentially, with more sensory awareness.

A career in semiconductor engineering followed. The energy and action of electrons brought a new dimension to my thinking through day-to-day observations of the unobservable by way of complex measurement techniques. While developing new computer-chip designs, I began to feel that we used an innate "intelligence" within atomic structure to create an image of our own mental function.

Yet, as I approached retirement, I had still not integrated and engaged the shimmering stump as bodily knowing and had missed the most important connection. I got another wake-up call, another imposition on my reality consciousness, in Cleveland, Ohio. After my move there, a kind man was helping me move boxes. He had recently had surgery for carpal tunnel syndrome, and this activity was not appropriate for his healing. When we had finished and were relaxing by watching a televised baseball game, a shared passion, he complained that his hand hurt. As he stretched it to me, I saw that several stitches had pulled out and the palm was red and swollen. Instinctively placing my hand over the wound, I felt as though my hand stuck to his hand. Next came the sensation that my hand had somehow interpenetrated his hand. I had an impulse to yank my arm back in fear. My upper-arm muscles could have pulled back, but that impulse passed instantly. A deeper knowing said that it was okay and I could remove it gently at the right time. So, I waited. I asked him if he felt anything strange, and he said that he felt a vibration in my hand. I did not feel a vibration. Part of our attention remained with the game. After ten or fifteen minutes, it felt right to carefully will my hand's energy boundary to separate from his, and I felt it obey. His wound had become only a hairline scar. All pain, swelling, and redness were gone. We had no words, no frame of reference, to deal with the experience. Focus safely stayed on the game's score.

Neither of us spoke of what had happened for two weeks. Then he asked, "If you can do that to me, what could you do if you got angry with me?" I appreciated his articulating his fear. I sensed that love empowered whatever had happened, but I had no response. I had not consciously chosen to create the experience. It was time to engage a spiritual director.

A very grounded person had witnessed and shared the experience, and a televised baseball game did not seem like a medium of deep hypnosis. With no clue as to how to integrate this experience into my reality, I hoped it was a onetime thing. I told my spiritual director that I thought this was an aberration and it would probably not happen again, but he sent people to see me who were ill and in pain, and healing happened many times.

I began studying energy medicine—first Reiki and then other modalities. For the first time, I began to connect my understanding of physics—all matter as vibrating light and energy, my shimmering stump experience—to my own body as energy. I felt like a dunce for having missed that connection for so long. That split in my awareness between knowledge and self-knowing was another point worthy of attention as I tried to discern a broken path for human awareness.

These two experiences taught me to follow the energy, as well as my normal sensory input, and to give deep attention to it as a real dimension of experience. They also taught me that boundaries are choices—personal choices, evolutionary choices, community choices, political choices, choices of the heart and of the hand, choices about energy and intention. Freedom is the knowledge that all these choices are held in love in a shared consciousness. We have so much freedom of choice in how we show up as human beings in the world. No matter the outcome of the evolutionary journey, human beingness is a wondrous experience!

INTRODUCTION

This is not a scientific treatise. Many pieces of a working hypothesis deserve to be examined. I am presenting an idea about a human wholeness that we've lost and are ready to reclaim. But that reclamation involves a process of reunification. Writing and reading, as a linear left-brain function, cannot easily serve that process well. The reader could, in fact, use this book to serve the separation by creating new definitions and thought compartments to reinforce our dichotomized thinking. Herein both the poetry and the science may irritate you. They poke each other. They want to simultaneously engage the attention of both sides of our brain and have them find themselves in each other. The reader can experience this with nagging frustration or integrating challenge. To fully share in the writer's experience, the reader will do both.

This book has three parts.

In chapters 1–5, I celebrate and explore gravity, touch, and shared energy as creative sources in our evolution, as fonts for our uniquely human nature. I've structured these chapters to encourage connection of the body, feelings, and the mind in remembering our origins, a journey from grooming to language. Shared myth has been well used for this purpose, but myth has also been used to disconnect from experience, to hide from the truth of compromising choices. In invitation, my words can only suggest my felt reality and hopefully offer a few arrows along a path of personal exploration of the deep, primal echoes in the soul.

Chapters 6–8 of the book focus on herding, especially shepherding in the Middle East, and the shifts in human consciousness that accompanied it. The herder's thinking and belief systems have had profound effects on Western civilization. In the herding experience, we can find the wound of separation between the masculine and feminine consciousness in each of us. The Hebrew and Christian scriptures give insight into both the gifts and wounds from that seminal herding experience. The understanding that can emerge from confronting herding choices may offer a key to freeing the masculine human soul from a heavy load of fear. Through projection and identification, how we managed sheep and cattle has reflected back into our self-assessment and shaped our human culture with cruelty as well as wealth. In this section, I keep to my own culture because that is what I know intuitively, and I do not try to project onto other cultures. By that choice, I do not suggest these ideas are confined to just Western culture.

The third part is about healing, reclamation, and reattunement. We can use touch and shared energy for healing while controlling contagion. We have "paid attention" to some things by shutting other things completely out of our attention. We ignored our breath, our most basic connection to life, as we industrialized and citified. Our growth carried both a high price and very great rewards. As we mature emotionally, I believe that we can learn to hold *both-and* rather than *either-or* and thus reclaim much of what we have paid for our progress this far. Section three shares some ideas for holding a more open attention that invites perception on several levels: our ego, our sensate self, and the shared consciousness. Perhaps as we regain the comfort and benefits in the shared energy of touch, we'll transcend isolating personal space, not only reclaiming what was lost but growing it with new intentionality. Unity consciousness is not something we can "get." It will always surprise us with new creativity. But we can recognize that we are always playing in it. We can grow in talent and insight for searching the both-and spaciousness of it all. It is my prayerful intention that this book be an instrument for nurturing wholeness, harmony, and radiance in our evolving human consciousness.

CHAPTER 1

Gravity as Love

In the last years of architect Buckminster Fuller's life, he gave a talk at IBM in Vermont. It was there I first heard his proposition that gravity and love are manifestations of the same force. The idea enthralled me. In my memory, he did not try to define a relationship between the two, such as gravity as a manifestation of love, or love as a manifestation of gravity. He simply invited the connection. Similarly, I had chosen to believe the statement "God is love" (1 John 4:8 RSV) early in adulthood. It was not an intellectual belief. I did not understand either word, but the connection called to my heart and felt true to my human experience. Buckminster Fuller's vision deepened that experiential knowing. My mind could attach to the connection as something my body already knew.

That small attraction between every atom in the universe, increasing exponentially with nearness, provides the perfect balance between unity and separateness that calls forth all form. *Gravity* had been a word, a scientific construct that I had compartmentalized in my mind, a shield from mystery, and a parameter for control. Now, its true power, with all its glorious subtleties, shined in my awareness. With maturity, love has become for me less about a concept, less about feeling and doing, and more about pure, open presence. The convolution of God, love, and gravity becomes more real every day.

I find great joy in the simple fact that I can feel it. I experience gravity in every moment. It is presence itself. I do not have to remember that God is gravity/love. I know it in my bones and muscles. I am physically aware of being held in a vast potential of relationship. Gravity/love becomes a field within which I am always learning to live more gracefully, or with more wild authenticity, or with a fresh new point of equilibrium between unity and separateness. Gravity is an enlivening, dynamic force, always teasing out some new relationship, some new potential and longing for interaction, and some new ground from which material form can show up with new expression. With its pull, it also creates pressure, creative pressing along with pulling, and creative expression—as a rising mountain range, as a sprouting seed, as expanding heart energy—the hand of God always felt supporting and beckoning into some new association, inviting a new creative connection.

Gravity holds us with eternal constancy. Ancient celebrations of cycle and season recognized the power of love in the dependability of these mysterious cycles. Life comes forth out of a dynamic and complex system of the sun, the moon, waves, wind, agglomeration and separation, and growth and decay. Gravity creates and recreates balances that exchange energy and information across countless shifting boundaries. Yet within all the subtle and the cataclysmic changes, there is the recognition of constancy. We have named that constancy *gravity*, and in naming of mystery, we have dismissed our awe and limited our mind's encounter with *what is*.

Gravity clasps a beautiful, flowing sea of air to our planet's surface and inflates our lungs, breathing into us our first, last, and every breath. We are breathed gently into being, breathing love and breathed by love. A constant rhythm of the breath, the blood, and the waves begets the experience of time. Gravity creates the time-space grid within which we can encapsulate an *I* within our consciousness. The hand of God is the hand of gravity, holding us with constancy in a subtly shifting creative field that invites the dance of relationship between unity and separateness; that invites us into love as a field of creative energy.

Gravity/love's foundational space-time grid provides our lives and consciousness with the linear and cyclic dimensions in which to experience, remember, anticipate, and envision. It maintains place, granting the power of directed growth and movement, of expectation and dream. Things mainly stay where we put them. We can stack stone to create a sheltering structure and know with great certainty—and trust—that it will stay there for many tomorrows. It enables and supports our actions in our environment. It grants us power to create boundaries of our own devising. What an amazing gift to know that things will stay put or move with a predictable constancy—to own a feeling of agency in our environment! We can create structure, organize our life, and build our personal and community life within the constancy of gravity's rhythms. Its constancy begets our free will. The space-time grid that underpins our entire conceptualization of cosmic order is built around our trust in gravity. Gravity provides a power for the nurturance of life and creativity so beyond comprehension that perhaps we must take it for granted and compartmentalize it in bits and pieces for the sake of our functionality.

We talk about love as a passion and a tender feeling, love as action in support of the other, but to be present to love as an energy field within which we continually refine our balance, learning to live deeper and deeper in the creative exploration of relationship, is a hugely ecstatic proposition in its immediacy. Entering Buckminster Fuller's perception of love and gravity as manifestations of the same force, *love* as a verb becomes a gentle sensitivity to balance, an easy awareness of holding both unity and separateness in a way that allows creativity to flourish. Love as a feeling becomes a spacious allowing, a dance of spontaneity, a trust in constancy's rhythm. We can feel the space in between as a pregnant holy space, gravid and heavily laden with potential.

Returning home from Fuller's talk, I asked my teenage son what he thought about the notion that love and gravity are aspects of the same force. He immediately responded, "You mean they both keep you down?" My son wanted to fly, pilot his own life free of parental concern. From his adolescent perspective, gravity and love impeded his emerging ego's need for mastery. He focused on the future and his aspirations. He took the past for granted, and the present was just not good enough compared to his dreams. This is a state of awareness very appropriate for adolescence, and one in which most of us continue to struggle. It has a developmental usefulness for claiming our freedom. In this example, gravity/love pressures us to move beyond our current boundaries—a pressure for self-expression. As gravity's pressure pushes up the mountains, as the clouds pile high in pressure fronts that deliver rain, and as the swelling seed is pushed up, our species, too, feels a pressure to change and engage in an ever-new and renewing relationship with life.

With a narrow mental focus, we ignore the seamlessness of the whole. Gravity is named and thereby defined, and compartmentalized. The dominant left side of the brain finds power and comfort in classification, separating us from reality's fullness with the end of making it more manageable, of relieving the felt pressure. The illusion of power in condensing gravity into a sliver of a concept that we take for granted, devalue, and see as something to be overcome creates weakness. True power comes through engaging with gravity, humbly open to its vast potential. We gain strength and balance and learn that we can fly. When we consciously open up to its presence as gravity/love, our dreams may find new awareness of support.

In the early 1900s, people learned to fly airplanes. The Wright brothers and others who were totally in love with flight risked their lives and all their resources. They were willing to engage in a long, dangerous encounter with all this energy's subtleties because they trusted that it could and would support them in a new way. This depth of attention is love. Mechanical flight is an obvious and direct example. In truth, gravity/love is part of all encounters—tires meeting the road, houses creaking, trees spreading shade, hearts pumping.

Developing Dimensions in Consciousness

Mysterious ancient stones, or megaliths, are an example of forgotten meaning in our ancestors' first conscious, imaginative engagement with gravity. Megaliths—Stonehenge, the Dolmens in Russia, the Taulas in Spain, the standing stone circles in Ireland and Scotland, the Rujm el-Hiri in Israel—engender feelings of awe and are thought to mark sacred space. Our wonder at them usually involves speculation about the intention and purpose the Stone Age folk who erected them had for the megaliths—as graves, calendars, sacred gathering places, and so on. If we contemplate their awesomeness from an awareness grounded in gravity, the stones themselves hold the insight. Stones persisted in place, connecting hearts and souls to the future.

The growing edge for Neo- and Mesolithic people was their engagement with stone, as their label attests. Perceptions of divinity are most intense for communities and individuals at their expanding growth boundaries. For early prehistoric humans, the cycles of days and seasons shaped their experience of time. Permanence belonged to the realm of divinity, to the firmament, to the mountains, to all that seemed unchanging. Erecting massive stone structures attested to permanence. It gave man a way to participate with the divine in a grand linear arena of time that transcended the seasons, even the seasons of a man's life. The weightier the stone, the more profound the sense of permanence. History was born in man's relationship with stone. Human works could reach beyond the body, allowing man's power to become part of a future that stretched beyond his awareness. Stone megaliths connected with the human soul's desire to persist after death. Through the use of stone, our ancestors projected a godlike power for creating across linear time. The image of stone was gravid. The future opened as a canvas for creativity, imagination, and conquest. This new agency within a linear time dimension was a seminal and weighty conceptual evolution they formed through engaging with gravity and stone. History was born. The amazing feats of engineering and generations of effort that went into creating early megaliths attest to the importance of the human soul's experience of causality within linear time. Humans could entertain a dream of permanence. The *now* of the megalith builder populated both past and future. The human spirit challenged gravity with megaliths and penetrated into a linear time dimension.

Each buried seed's first knowing as it opens to growth is *up*, informed by gravity. I find it fascinating to contemplate how trees informed the development of our humanity. Trees are magnificent manifestations of life dancing with gravity, demonstrating height, balance, symmetry, and strength. From Druidism to the Tree of Life, the "wholiness" of trees' role in our becoming human is a delight to remember. The safety of their upper reaches gave us a heavenly place for rest. Transcendence, the perspective from above the fray, was an embodied thought pattern and experiential lesson that trees taught to our ancestors. It has been preserved as a primal spiritual desire within human consciousness.

The fine-tuning of balance in treetops, the development of core muscle strength from climbing the trunks, and the expansion in perspective afforded by height are some ways trees encouraged and enabled a new upright posture for our primate ancestors. Trees taught us how to settle into a new center of gravity from which wondrously complex experience could evolve. A heightened perspective over distance allowed us to plan responses to approaching threat. Sightings of far-off danger granted a time delay—an opening in time and space in which to use timing as part of a considered response and the new neural pathways to manage planned choices. Love of a wider, heightened perspective is inherent in our humanity. Large vistas feed our souls. Trees still provide an energetic, spiritual support to our vertical orientation to gravity. Embedded in our minds' structure are permanent patterns for perception and thought—hierarchy, transcendence, heaven, spiritual ascendency, and higher education. Implied inherent value ascribed to the vertical dimension shapes our reality and our identification with tree's wisdom.

Conscious Attunement

Now, let us turn from looking at our past growth and play with the possibilities in a conscious engagement with gravity/love and God in the present moment. Many people have honed a conscious attunement to their breath and thus experienced the vivid connection to self, life, and wholeness that can result. Can consciously sensing the gravitational field create similar results? Can it open our sensitivity to relationship potential in ourselves and in our environment?

Our neuromuscular systems constantly engage with gravity in careful, precise sensitivity. In myriad other ways, every cell of our fluid-filled being moves and engages in its embrace. Bringing gravity into our mental constructs of reality is an act of loving solidarity between mind and body. Grounding our conscious awareness in gravity can impart a holistic perspective and cultivate subtle awareness of new potential in awareness. Love becomes a field of energy that embraces and supports all in the moment, not something sought after, nor a scripted action. Trust in life's support, and the rhythms of its constancy can permeate each moment of awareness. The intimate, immediate joy of the dancer, attuned in spatial awareness, holding the rhythm in both body and mind, feeling the energy connection in the space between—we can access all of this in all movement and in all stillness. We can feel gravity hold us and love open us to our true, essential beauty as part of a connected whole.

Playing in Gravity

Start by just lifting your limbs or head and feeling the pull. Sense life as being lived within love, a concrete awareness of living in Earth's gravitational field. Sense that we are held with reliable constancy, with trust that reassures each of our movements. Lying down to sleep, we snuggle into being held reliably through the night and awaken safely in our bed—a priceless gift. One simple, powerful encounter can happen when we sense the buoyancy that gravity's hold supplies to us in the atmosphere. As gravity holds us to the earth, it also constantly buoys us within the fluid atmosphere. It lessens the effort needed to stay erect. It is a small effect when compared to that felt in water, and we make no note of it in our usual awareness. We've long forgotten the experience since our toddler selves played in the sea of air and slowly learned the fine motor and sensory sensitivity for balance. As we walk the earth, we are supported subtly in our effort to remain erect. Stand with your feet slightly apart in front of a chair back or something to catch yourself if you overbalance. Lean gently forward. On the edge of your balance, you can sense the buoyancy of the atmosphere supporting you; the same buoyancy that supports air travel and clouds.

Gravity carefully manages all the fluids that support us; our breath is part of the wind and our blood part of the cycle of water from cloud to sea. Attuning ourselves to these experiences consciously expands our awareness in unexpected ways. To learn to consciously live within love by attuning yourself to the gravitational field is to learn to gracefully move through life with great trust. It calls all atoms of earth into constant change and rebalance. Within gravity's force, the elements of earth, air, fire, and water interact constantly, enabling and challenging life, and maintaining a vibrant, creative dance.

Ah! Reminders of the full meaning of gravity flow through our language in some of its most energy-filled words, like *gravid*, *grace*, *gratitude*, and *grave*. A little etymological exploration can help us recall the forgotten experiential connections that sourced our abstraction of gravity/love. These words all stem from the ancient Indo-European base *gwer-*.[1] The multiple definitions of *grace* all point toward a tremendous active energy, a celebration of the beauty our species feels when moving in time and space and supported by gravity/ love: "beauty or charm of form, composition, movement or expression"; "a sense of what is right and proper"; "the unmerited love and favor of God for mankind"; "a title of respect or reverence"; "divine influence acting in a

[1] *Gwerə-* is a Proto-Indo-European root; its meanings include "heavy," "favored," and "important." *Webster's New World College Dictionary*. 4th ed. Cleveland, OH: Wiley, 2010.

person"; "to adorn"; "temporary exemption"[2]; a grace period; a short prayer of gratitude for a meal and more. The list of definitions gives a rich testament to right relationship, or equivalently to attunement to gravity. As we engage with gravity as love, it grants us new grace, and we grow in grace as we allow it to attune us to subtle relationships. We dance, and we are danced. We breathe, and we are breathed. We have the grace to be present. We encounter ourselves and all creation as gravid, pregnant and swollen with a weighty burden of eggs, of relational potential awaiting some new fullness of creative expression.

When we encounter awesome beauty, our minds may go to gratitude or to prayer as deliberate responses. Or they may try to analyze why and how the experience pleases us and to seek words to describe and share the experience. Or we may look for the best angle and lighting to preserve the memory in a photograph. All these responses are appropriate, but somehow, they can leave us with a hollow place inside, echoing with an odd loneliness our words and images can't satisfy. By tuning into love as our gravitational field, we can reclaim the totality of the experience and be enfolded in the grace of the moment. If we allow gravity to simply hold us grounded and secure in this moment's awe, we feel our bodies settle as the fluid in every cell responds in unity. If we consciously breathe, letting gravity fill our lungs, the inspiration can claim us for the moment of encounter. Gravity/love will claim us in unity with all that we sense in the moment. We know ourselves and our experience as part of the whole. Thus do we release our role as detached observer and enter a fullness of experiential unity. Allowing our perception to seed within this field of gravity/love grows rich connections with all we encounter. The dimensions of conscious presence expand.

Mystics and gurus dedicate long hours to meditation, prayer, and other spiritual practices with the hope of awakening to the pure energetic dimensions beyond the boundaries of ordinary consciousness. They generally agree that only grace opens us up to sensing transcendent energy fields with open, unconditioned, nonjudgmental awareness. Preparation through the conscious practice of open attention can be fruitful, but not necessarily a precondition, nor a sure path, to such experience. We do not usually see awareness of gravity as a transcendent experience. But can it be a very grounded basis for expanded awareness? It is an energy field and, as such, a component of all energy fields. By cultivating a conscious awareness of

---

[2] *Webster's New World College Dictionary.* 4th ed. Cleveland, OH: Wiley, 2010.

gravity, can we give our minds and bodies both permission and schooling for coming into awareness of other energy fields? If we experience gravity as love, we will also experience it with love—with an open heart to all of life. I submit that this simple practice can open us to avenues of grace that illuminate ordinary existence, not just ecstatic moments.

Sensing into gravity as the ground of our experience is a practice of presence. It is an opening to the subtleties of relationship in the moment. The awareness of gravity as love allows us to choose in any moment to return to the comfort of womb love and the inherent joy of relationship and trust— as the moment we remember our original self. Let me share some poetic reflections on gravity and love.

Henry and Theodore

I met old Henry when he was about sixty.
The story was that his back was broken as a child
And he had simply been put to bed to heal.
He was a hunchback, bent nearly double,
And the years brought his hands ever closer to the earth.
He always worked, mentioning no pain,
And since his face was always lowered,
No one saw if it was so.
He would turn his face sideways when he spoke,
Giving only a scant profile and looking quickly away
As if afraid of seeing pity in your glance.
He worked as a farmhand for Theodore.
Theodore's wife, Edith, who usually won out,
Didn't think Henry worth much as a farmhand.
But Theodore kept him on into their seventies,
Until Theodore's death.
One day shortly before that event, I was in the hardware store.
Theodore and Henry walked in together, both bent
With hands inches from the floor, talking softly.
Approaching the counter, Theodore straightened and made his request.
Then he bent back over as they waited.

Opening to Gravity

Its presence expands in awareness,
Bursting and flowering
Out of the small box into which it was stuffed.
A new lightness of being
(That box was so weighty!),
A fullness of grace,
All movement is now gravid,
Even the bending of old age,
Womb love drawing me back
To the center
To the grave.

CHAPTER 2

Forelimbs and Transcendence

One night, while falling asleep, I experienced a very crisp sensation. I felt a large feathered wing covering me. In that moment, I knew in my bones that angels had once been embodied, and that large feathered wings had special significance to their sojourn as corporal beings.

The next morning's newspaper included an article on a discovery that some dinosaurs likely had four-chambered hearts and were warm-blooded. Previously, I had read that scientists had identified birds as genetic evolutionary offshoots of dinosaurs. When I connected this information to my experience, it suggested a new possibility, and I enjoyed making a big leap. Perhaps in cosmic consciousness, in unity consciousness, the spirits of angels express some realization of the evolutionary potential that dinosaurs and birds achieved. What fun to contemplate!

Themes of angels, dragons, and dinosaurs are prominent in our cultural memory and all worth pondering and appreciating. Are they connected? The dinosaur image, once menacingly reptilian, has transformed to include the lovable character, Barney, a symbol of love, joy, and comfort for our children. Dragons and large serpents populate mythology around the globe. Breath of fire symbolizes rapid, fierce transformative power that both destroys and magically creates. Could there be a connection between rapid (in evolutionary time scales) evolution or development and warm-bloodedness? Creatures began generating more intense internal fire as their hearts expanded to four chambers. Did that fire, the heart's intensified energy, physically express a desire for new relationships in and with the world? Did that desire become as much an evolutionary determinant as survival? Did love become a physically manifested power to influence the flow of evolution with a force of directed desire? Could the dragon's breath of fire symbolize the power of an increased passion for life that came with a four-chambered heart?

The evolution of dinosaurs into the feathered, flying avian creatures that so charm our senses marks an amazing transformative feat of evolutionary creativity. Lumbering massiveness to gravity-defying lightness could suggest a spiritual journey to freedom and transcendence. After the cataclysmic meteor collision that presumably ended the dinosaur era in fire and ash, a phoenix rose from the ashes—a dinosaur/bird. Could we interpret that evolution as a spiritual transformation? Could dinosaur/birds have embodied the spiritual entities that we now name *angels*? The expanding reptilian consciousness relentlessly sought safety in transcendence, evolving clawed forelimbs into wings—such may well be the spiritual consciousness translated for us now as angels.

The Challenge of Gravity

A commonality between dinosaur–bird and primate–human evolution is the major transformation of forelimbs. Both demonstrated amazing creativity in their adaptations to gravity. I project that a commonality between these two evolutionary paths was the heart's fire of desire to reach for what lies just beyond—that the dramatic change in forelimbs' powers resulted from a desire for expanded domains. Dinosaur/birds' wings grew in a new relationship with gravity. Their forelimbs played with gravity over myriad generations, occupying new environs on the edge of the old that challenged their experience of connection to earth, air, fire, and water. The safety in treetops allowed for song and colorful plumage, bold expressions of desire. A very valid question to ask is this: How much of that evolutionary journey did desire power—a desire they expressed in persistent habitation of challenging environs and in sexual choice? Offspring learned to fly, to live above the earth in trees, and to find safety in transcendence. Did a desire for transcendence empower the change? Was life on the ground not good enough? Was it energetically satisfying to play with gravity (playfulness) and discover its subtler powers? Does gravity/love itself create a force for new forms to emerge on earth—a force often felt as dissatisfaction with the current boundaries? Did the dinosaur/bird journey generate a consciousness of universal creative power that now shows up in our shared unity consciousness as angelic energy, or an energy of worship?

The path of human evolution involved a similar stretch toward transcendence, but with a very immanent texture. We reached for each other in community and cooperation and for tools to reshape our shared space. The patterns of possibility in our hands and brains also emerged from a new relationship with gravity. We stretched within our new erectness to play further with gravity to build and shape, to suspend shelters around us, to connect in time and space in ever-larger community, and recently to fly by means of our dexterous creativity. The evolutionary journeys of primates/humans and dinosaurs/birds share a radical and rapid transformation, powered by the fire in the heart that forelimbs expressed. Forelimbs are within the heart's energy field, a seat of passion and desire, an energy field that is shared in community.

Defensive adaptation to ensure survival does not seem to have adequately empowered the speed and scope of the evolutionary path of either dinosaur/birds or primate/humans. The desire for transcendence and for safety above the earth's surface appears to have informed the bird's evolutionary path. Human forelimb evolution demonstrates a desire for community and immanence, and for intimate interaction with the earth to recreate our environment with tools and cooperation. Note that the element of reaching for the new implies some dissatisfaction with the status quo in both scenarios.

Combining reptilian and bird images invites us into the mystery of our creature identity, the contrasts of limitation and possibility, immanence and transcendence, and danger and delight. Primal reptilian knowing is unity awareness at its essence, the transformation of energy by eating and being eaten. Unity consciousness at the level of our intellect is probably impossible, but our reptilian brain lives in just that space. Meditation lets our intellect recollect that sense of unity without actually encountering its reality in surrendering individual form. The reptilian brain holds the most ancient wisdom about life and unity, about our true essence as a transformational process.

An Exercise in Unity and Transcendence

In the Gospel of Matthew 10:16, Jesus instructs his followers to be "wise as serpents and harmless as doves."[3] I have found that we can best explore the meaning in these words on the energetic level with an in-depth meditation that senses into the experience of being first the serpent and then the bird.

I invite you to read through the following and then try to identify with both species' energy as a meditative exercise. Be open to encountering the creative flow of power within each without fear or judgment. Know your abandonment into this sensory identification as a form of prayer.

Lying prone would be a fitting way to begin with the serpent. Start at the feet, and imagine a kind of rippling motion up your body as it enters an awareness of gravity holding you in contact with the surface that supports you. With deep breathing, bring an intention to listen to your spinal column and to sense into your vibration, listening with the whole body. With the breath, slowly retract power from the limbs, first arms and then legs, pulling it back into the core and wrapping all the power around your spinal column. Feel the sinuous fluidity as the spine flexes. Let gravity hold you flattened against the earth, aware of each texture against scaled skin. Feel each sensation as part of the self—no inside or outside. The earth's smells envelop you, a cloud of richly textured smells and tastes. This cloud is yours. You cannot separate from it. It is part of you. Feel the temperature of the earth you rest on. You perfectly share the heat energy that melts and moves, with no felt boundary. You are the earth, the rock, and the water that you move over or within. All that enters your awareness is you. There is no other. You are whatever is within your perceptual awareness. You recognize prey as part of you when you first perceive it. Capturing it marks the start of the digestive process. The vibrations in the earth are you. The wind that sends the faintest tremor down into the tree root beneath you—its movement is yours. Nothing acts on or against you, for all that you perceive is already you. You are all the vibrations, all the odors, all the textures on your skin. You know earth as yourself. Your movement flows, informed by all your earth self. With no other, no conflict, and no fear, and with a rich, undifferentiated perceptual awareness, you are beingness with fluid, fine-tuned response ability. Trust in being; unclouded wisdom about the essence of life is yours. There is no boundary between

---

[3] American Standard Version.

life and death—only transformation. When you have explored this as far as you would like, bring the power back into your limbs. Feel your human boundaries, and enjoy them.

Next, imagine yourself as a bird. Transforming into a bird celebrates buoyancy, transcendence, and spaciousness. Standing now, let the bones lighten to delicate, hollow bones, for the flight-over-fight choice was made generations ago. With all the heart's and forelimbs' energy, surrender to the single-minded desire to embrace the wind. Release all desire to touch and manipulate anything but air. For this moment, abandon all desire to hold, text, or create with the hands. Surrender to reaching for air, sensing its movement and buoyancy. Release all need to defend or aggress from the forelimbs except the power to beat the air; demand its support. Release all desire to sense and perceive with the hands except the knowing of layers of wind—flow, current, and pressure. All the heart's and forelimbs' energy stands ready to catch wind's playfulness.

Long ago, scales extended out as feathers, separate, delicate, and overlapping to tickle the wind, sense its power and wildness, and trap its power as your own. Its flow is yours to enter and leave, to struggle against or ride, and to rest on or play with in exuberance. Your fire is within you, belonging to you, conserved in light, fluffy inner feathers, a downy comforter. Your love of heat and radiance calls you to fly free for long days and distances, pursuing the sun. With a fast-paced heart and quick, energetic movements, you must build your nest with a hardened beak mouth, with forelimbs reserved for soaring. Far-sighted eyes survey expanding vistas for food, enemies, and partners. With no fear of summoning predators, you can fill the safety of distance and separation from earth with song. Your perch is high. Perspective, song, and lightness of being are yours. When you have savored the safety and freedom of swimming through the atmosphere to some satisfaction, land back on earth. Remember and sense deeply into how your current human embodiment is held and supported by a field of gravity/love potential. Lift your arms, feeling their weight, and let your hands dance in the air, listening to them express their creative connection to gravity's loving constancy.

Our ancient evolutionary heritage holds both unity and transcendence, oneness and separateness. They are all ours. We must hold their wisdom consciously and begin to stay present to the trade-offs. Holding unity and transcendence as ideals, as an otherness to which we aspire and strive, creates an inflation of separation that betrays reality and a differentiation from earth that becomes insane. They are patterns of awareness that conjoin in our internal structure. They cradle our essence in our dance with boundaries; the boundaries we honor, we snuggle into, we struggle against, we strain to surpass, and we dare approach only in fantastic dreams all hold out to us fresh relationship in a field of gravity/love.

Forelimbs are fired up in the heart space. In the space of an open heart, both differentiation and unity spin in the dynamic dance of creation, where love dances with self as other. This is the pain that undergirds the creative magic flowing into the hands. We can best consciously know and remember otherness in the missteps that expand our projections. Wisdom engages both the unity and the transcendence of our embodiment at the hard, contradictory edges, limits, and conflicts. The boundaries of concentrated energy potential within matter yield in fluidity to gravity/love, remembering. Grief is held in the trough and gratitude in the crest of the wave, the same energy of valuing reoriented in time and space, the energy of unconditional love requiring unconditional change. In the next chapter, we will explore some boundaries engaged by human hands, currently the most powerful instruments of change on this planet.

CHAPTER 3

Energies in Shared Fields

This section derives from the personal foundational experiences I described in the introduction, the "shimmering stump" and "baseball healing" experiences that shaped my appreciation and wonder at boundary experiences. I gave more conscious attention to my hands, and they shared a new awareness of life all their own. I came to see them as more than just tools or instruments. They had knowledge and wisdom—their own sense of a subtle reality that they wanted to teach my conscious mind; and so they did, leading me into a healing role.

When my hands touched a body who desired help, I felt communication on a cellular level. Sensations in my hands gave me clear hints about the quality of the distress that the cells felt, and about the emotional and spiritual energy they held, as well as their physical condition. My hands could help distressed cells remember wholeness. I felt energy pass both to and from others' cells and into my hands. This energy was not sourced in my body but through it. The transfer did not deplete my energy. It increased it. My loving intentions were honored and guided as I explored the boundaries, and as others healed, so did I. I accepted my sensations and intuition as hints—hints that I was capable of misinterpreting.

Experience taught me that healing is a gift like musical talent. I learned from other healers and taught others to explore their own healing energy. All caring people have this capacity in some form. Its quality and intensity vary in similar ways to musical talents, varying in tone and range; some are highly gifted, some specialized, some best expressed in certain instruments or ranges. To use that power, one only need touch another or oneself as if touching a newborn, without judgment, expectation, or agenda—with only awe at a boundless potential for new wholeness. From this state of mind and heart, helpful information may arise in the mind, or it may not, but wise energy will flow in the body.

After World War II, an academic and medical interest in touch arose, sparked by the discovery of the severe damage that arose in neglected children who spent their infancy in orphanages in Romania.[4] Nathan A. Fox studied this phenomenon for years at the University of Maryland. Ashley Montagu of Princeton wrote a landmark book on touch, first published in 1971, in which he discusses the skin as "the exposed portion of the nervous system"[5] and analyzes the physiological, developmental, cultural, anthropological, and emotional components of touch. He includes the topic of therapeutic touch in an appendix. The *failure to thrive* syndrome in warehoused orphans is a widely accepted example of not only the power but the necessity of loving touch. Without touch, we cannot access the patterns of wholeness for growth. These patterns are a shared knowing of being human.

I'll define *subtle energy* as energy that we have not yet learned to detect or define on the level of shared discourse within our culture. We can sometimes intuit this form of energy and bring the experience to a conscious level by interpreting it in concepts and words we learned from other prior experience. We live within a sea of many energy fields. Energy fields have structure. Energy fields carry information. Energy fields carry the mathematical intelligence for form. Sound waves move through the air with amplitude and direction. Images move through the atmosphere on signal waves to our TVs. Cells in our eyes and brains detect and interpret the information in the visible spectrum of light waves with individual variation. Infrared energy waves cause the atoms in our skin to vibrate faster, transferring warmth. Subtler waves surround and permeate us, carrying millions of simultaneous conversations, which cell phones encode and decode. Waves of energy have

---

[4] Nelson, Charles A., Nathan A. Fox, and Charles H. Zeanah. *Romania's Abandoned Children: Deprivation, Brain Development, and the Struggle for Recovery.* Cambridge, MA: Harvard University Press, 2014.

[5] Montagu, Ashley. *Touching: The Human Significance of the Skin.* New York: Perennial Library, 1986, p. 5.

a range over which they dissipate as they get farther from their source. Their signal strength (or *amplitude*) depends on their distance from their source.

Energy and matter, we now know, are interchangeable, which means that energy fields of some type are inherent to all the matter that surrounds us. An energy field is the range in time and space of some effect or some influence produced just by *being*. Its detection can cause problems for our consciousness. Evolutionary choices have determined our sensory receptivity. Carl Jung discussed a shared unconscious as an energy field that holds our species' past experience.[6] We can question its existence because the field itself is currently undetectable. But its existence explains some human cognitive phenomena that are otherwise unexplainable. An analogous situation is the memory of identity and experiences that persists in our bodies while our individual cells die and are replaced many times during our lifetime. The probability that unknown energy fields exist in all material form is such that the unscientific approach is to dismiss it without exploration.

The community of cells that are a human body display functions of mind-boggling complexity in their cooperation and almost instantaneous communication. It is a highly energized organizational system. Its functions have energy fields associated with them that extend out beyond the skin. Some we have learned to detect with technology, such as EKGs and EEGs. Transportation of information by wave energy rather than by particles has obvious advantages. It is less intrusive, and its passage can occur transparently except to its specialized detectors.

Let's consider some possibilities that can happen when wave energy fields from two individuals overlap or intermingle. Within the body are detectors for whatever energy fields the body produces. That only makes sense. We know about some and are learning more all the time about others, but some likely exist about which we have no conscious knowledge at all—but our cells know and use the information. Whatever detector has evolved in one person will likely present itself in the rest of the species, but like with all our organs, individuals may have differing sensitivity levels or response times. Thus, our cells can detect and respond to energy that is not self-produced when they are in close proximity to another body.

---

[6] Jung, Carl G. *The Collected Works of C. G. Jung, Volume 9, Part 1: Archetypes and the Collective Unconscious*. Translated by Gerhard Adler and R. F. C. Hull. Princeton, NJ: Princeton University Press, 1969.

The most powerful effects in the shared energy experience happen when the waves of overlapping energy fields synchronize at the same frequency, with the waves' peaks and valleys coinciding. If the peaks in one person's energy wave coincide and synchronize with the peaks of another person's overlapping energy wave, the combined energy goes up exponentially—the energies not just adding together but multiplying. So take an example that ignores units and just talks ratios: If a wave with a height of two has an energy of four (2^2), then a wave with a height of three has an energy of nine (3^2). When they come together in phase (synchronized), they would have a combined height of five, but their combined energy would be twenty-five (5^2).

In a shared experience, each person's cellular detectors for that energy receive a much, much larger hit than their usual individual experience. We have all experienced mood changes when we are with someone; we have all experienced a shift to either higher or lower levels of well-being, safety, joy, fear, and contentment, or simply felt energized by another's company. These real experiences are so familiar we take them for granted. Our energy shifts with the introduction of another's energy field into our space. We literally build on each other's experience. Group mind or team effort when energy synchronizes creates far more than the sum of its parts. In most safe situations, our bodies enjoy this energy sharing and coordinate, like sharing in a dance.

Eastern medicine has traditionally structured its concepts of health and disease around energy, defining both a chakra system within the body, which organizes the body's energy in an ascending order that reflects evolutionary development, and a meridian system, which plots the energy paths within the body.[7] Chakra and meridian systems have been used for centuries to describe the body's energy structure. In other cultures, subtle energy is known by other names, including *qi, chi, prana, kundalini, orgone,* and *mana.* Energy-healing modalities evolve in all cultures. In *Vibrational Medicine* (3rd ed.),[8] Richard Gerber gives an excellent summary of current and ancient theory and practice.

From the ground of my own experience with shared energy fields, I would like to propose a theory that the regular physical touch of primate grooming was key to the evolution of human consciousness. This is not

---

[7] Brennan, Barbara Ann. *Hands of Light.* New York: Bantam, 1988.

[8] Gerber, 2001, *Vibrational Medicine (3rd ed.)* Rochester,VT.,Bear&Co.

at all an attempt at a scientific proof but an attempt to "follow the energy" back to possible sources. The following chapters will express wonderings, questions, and propositions about how the primate-grooming experience and its subsequent loss have informed human development and continue to challenge us.

CHAPTER 4

Grooming

With the recognition of the power of shared energy fields, an idea entered my heart and mind that primate-grooming behavior may have been a powerful factor in protohuman development. My approach here is to suggest a hypothesis that might help us understand ourselves and our peculiar mode of consciousness with new insight and wise compassion. I hope that it also suggests avenues that can renew our joy in life. We cannot know the complexities of our prehistoric path, so I do not attempt to prove a theory. Just trying to follow the energy of primal memory and patterns involves a fun exploration, especially if it adds room for kindness and delight to our self-image.

Standing Up to Fleas

Four million years ago, some primates shifted their center of gravity and stood erect. Thus, an energetic potential opened for far greater creativity than even the wondrous journey from reptile to bird. What had been underneath was now in front. The heart's energy field that had embraced earth moved to embrace a new spaciousness. The soft underbelly was exposed. Perspective changed. Group relationships shifted to accommodate the new open vulnerability by circling together. Primates sought support and protection in close, cohesive community. Forelimbs, freed for new possibility, chose more group intimacy. Fingertips, protected from the wear and tear of travel and body weight, grew in sensitivity with more nerve endings. As community circled tightly and intimately to fortify its boundaries, a thriving parasite population grew as a formidable byproduct. Forelimbs humbly went after the irritation that fleas caused. Did that activity seed human consciousness and culture? "Grooming is a form of touch that primates enjoy throughout their lives. It is far more than the simple exercise of cleaning and ridding the hair of external parasites; rather, it is a primary social glue that holds primate groups together, beginning with the bond between mothers and infants."[9]

Current theories about the development of our opposable thumbs trend toward clubbing, throwing, and using tools in hunting and defense as the major impetuses.[10] But itching is compelling. It grabs the attention. Perhaps the persistence of fleas was a powerful factor for generating adaptations for manual dexterity. Had thumbs developed from the cited activities, they might likely have more sex-linked characteristics. So it is worth considering that grooming as a shared immune response could have shaped the human hand as much or more than hunting and defending.

Beyond opposable thumbs, I would speculate that grooming provided a path toward many adaptations that define our human nature. A preschool curriculum would include most skills the grooming activity hones: eye–hand coordination; close, detailed observation; small motor development; focused attention at close range; and most especially awareness of reciprocity. (And, as an aside, could the way that many humans track their hand movement with their tongues have originated with the way primates eat fleas as the only sure way of disposing of them?)

For me, the strongest suggestion that grooming might be the source of our frontal-lobe development is that it involved split attention in a relaxed atmosphere. The frontal lobes are a relatively slow network compared to more primitive parts of the brain, a more flexible and adaptive network without the hardwiring of primitive survival function. This suggests that adaptations grew in response to complexity but not immediate threat, and that contemplative time itself was part of the experience that drove the frontal lobes' evolution.

---

[9] Jablonski, Nina G. *Skin: A Natural History*. Berkeley, CA: University of California Press, 2006, p. 107.

[10] Young, Richard W. "Evolution of the Human Hand: The Role of Throwing and Clubbing," Journal of Anatomy 202, no. 1 (2003): 165–174.

Within an attitude of relaxed contemplation, primates engaged in focused attentive gazing, adroit small-motor activity, and an attuned emotional awareness of the other. They divided attention between fleas and the grooming partner. Close physical proximity demanded an attuned sphere of awareness. To have vulnerability within range of tooth and claw required development of a sympathetic refinement in relationship skill—effectively, some manners that would minimize violent reactivity. The desire for future reciprocal grooming was the impetus not just for manners but for new mental projection along the time dimension, an extended cause-and-effect learning. Grooming exercised these three arenas of simultaneous attention; future reciprocal benefit, a dexterous eye–hand small-motor task, and sensitivity to another's emotional and sensory state. This simultaneity within a relaxed state seems to me a possible basis for the growth of consciousness in complex, flexible neural networks.

Grooming provided a potent opportunity to refine emotional relationships. What better arena for learning to treat others as you would wish to be treated? Perhaps the Golden Rule is not just a precept that emerged quite universally in human consciousness but the experiential seed that formed that very consciousness.

When you add the effects of shared energy fields into protohumans' grooming experience, the potential for conscious growth increases. Within a good grooming session, the groomer and groomed's breathing would have slowed and become synchronized. As bodies begin to follow each other in breath and heart rhythms, their energy fields gain coherence, and with synchronization, energy sharply increases in the overlapping fields of both bodies. Not all grooming sessions would have generated this experience, but when it happened, it would have been self-reinforcing. Bodies would have sought to recreate the experience when possible. When that synchronization happened, both would have felt more relaxed, healthier, and more open to shared sensations.[11] Whatever perceptual experiences they shared while holding a similar energy in both bodies could heighten that response or experience. Not every grooming session would achieve higher energy states, but when that did happen, the benefits would provoke a desire for more,

---

[11] Keverne, Eric B., Nicholas D. Martensz, and Bernadette Tuite. "Beta-Endorphin Concentrations in Cerebrospinal Fluid of Monkeys Are Influenced by Grooming Relationships," *Psychoneuroendocrinology* 14, no. 1–2 (1989): 155–161.

an intent to recreate the process again in the future—a contact high, so to speak. Healing benefits would accrue and enhance motivation. Slowly, the skill would have grown.

Refining the grooming experience into higher healing levels would have enhanced community survival, and those healing benefits may have modulated dominance instincts within the group. Quoting Nina Jablonski on touch, "This activity in turn stimulates the central nervous system, prompting the secretion of endogenous opiates (endorphins and related compounds that make us feel good). The result is both pleasure and relief, with measurable reduction of anxiety and stress levels and strengthening of the immune system, whose functioning is inhibited by high stress levels."[12] The dominant male would likely have consistently experienced the highest levels of stress from injury and from vigilance. Within the dominance hierarchy, he would have received the most grooming from male underlings. But as the skill developed, he might have instead sought attention from the best groomers. The opportunity to be groomed in a high-energy field would have provided rejuvenation and healing to the dominant male that supported him in the demands of his role and his body's survival.

Infanticide, a competitive tactic in primate dominance behavior, would have had a high price within the grooming system. It could create an emotional disruption that badly impacted the quality of the grooming experience. A mother's grief would have prevented a shared high-energy field. Keeping the good groomers happy had a survival benefit. Aggressiveness within the group could drain off healing energy when fear or another negative emotion prevented alignment within the shared fields. Special friendships and loyalties would have grown around good grooming experiences. Subtle new factors of emotional attunement and cultivation would have intruded on dominance power structures. Group solidarity came to depend on gentler forces that modulated dominance within the group but, make no mistake, did not displace dominance as the primary protective force for group structure and safety. A new dominance tactic around fostering alliances would have emerged.

Within observed primate communities, grooming is the social glue and a rather sacred ritual of forgiveness and reconciliation that the group

---

[12] Jablonski, Nina G. *Skin: A Natural History.* Berkeley, CA: University of California Press, 2006, p. 111.

encourages.[13] It has the power to moderate and shift the hormonal responses in a strained relationship, restoring energy fields to alignment with each other and the group after an altercation. It defines and renews group membership. Forgiveness physically releases negative emotional energy within the shared field as grooming relaxes both parties. Both perpetrator and victim benefit from aligning their fields in peace, as does the whole group. The goal of producing energy coherence and enhancing the shared field energy for healing and pleasure grows in value as a moderator of dominance instinct.

Strengthening immune systems for communal living by way of the enhanced energy fields makes it easier to live in larger packs and communities. That also may have helped balance the negative impact of increasing brain size on birth survival.

Shared energy fields are critical to herding mammals in their response to danger. By gathering into a close group, they increase the energy of their group's alarmed state so each mammal has more stamina, speed, and attunement to coordinated movement. When faced with predatory danger, they function as a whole with an exponential increase in shared energy.

Grooming is not triggered by a state of alarm. It is relaxed. The coordinated energy-field attunement that grooming occasions can be experienced slowly, and its subtler energy shifts can be probed. This experience of subtle energy that primates and protohumans enjoyed may have inherently fostered neocortical growth and slowly brought about tiny incremental increases in neural connection on a journey to consciousness. An enhanced shared energy field would have provided a potent source of creative power for learning a subtle energy attunement to the boundary between other and self. The foundation was laid at this sacred boundary for shared projections long before consciousness as we know it emerged. The presence of shared high-energy fields would have empowered and enhanced the special awareness of self and other, fed by the desire for reciprocity. Shared projections have great power, especially when they gain physical expression, such as in symbol or image. The current creative power of shared projection—found, for example, in religion and in monetary systems—began long before our first known examples in cave paintings and amulets.

The theologian Martin Buber posited the human psyche has an inherent

---

[13] De Waal, Frans. *Peacemaking among Primates*. Cambridge, MA: Harvard University Press, 1989.

"I-Thou" structure, which differs from the "I-It" structure of utility and survival. The I-Thou relationship holds a sense of mystery and awe (whether the *thou* is seen as divine, human, or both) that transcends survival issues and presents a pregnant creative spaciousness in awareness.[14] This special connection, which Buber felt was inherent in the mind, may result from our mental faculties having been cultivated within heightened energy fields of the grooming relationship. My attempts to explain this connection should not be seen as devaluing or demystifying. Probing the source of this intimate invitation into loving energy makes it no less a mystery. As with gravity, it is foolish to compartmentalize with verbal symbolism in the hopes of gaining control and some illusion of understanding. We do not understand gravity. We have gained some insight about interacting with the gravitational force, but we project a Gravitron and grapple with gravity's effects on time and space as we try to grasp its true mystery. If we acknowledge the universality of our connection through energy fields, it makes those fields no less mysterious. With insight, we gain the freedom to more actively and intentionally participate in this aspect of loving connection. I readily acknowledge that this has a risky learning curve that requires wisdom, but it seems to be our destiny, our special invitation as humans, to explore deep connections in consciousness.

Noam Chomsky[15] has a similar hypothesis that parallels Buber's, but on the linguistic level. He has posited that all language builds on a grammar structure inherent in our brains, a structure that makes it easy for children to learn language. Mental constructs for subject, object, and tense appear to exist organically as a base for connecting infinitely varied configurations of words in an easily understood manner in any language. I would submit that the grooming experience would have provided just such a structure for neocortical growth. The subject and object boundaries would have grown during lengthy grooming sessions. Identification and projection processes[16]

---

[14] Buber, Martin. *I and Thou*. Translated by Walter Kaufmann. New York: Scribner, 1970. Touchstone, 1996.

[15] Chomsky, Noam. *Language and Mind*. Cambridge, UK: Cambridge University Press, 2006.

[16] Identification involves seeing and imitating, taking in an image of another as part of the self. Projection involves the reverse—seeing a personal experience of the self as part of another. They are complementary imaginative processes.

would have developed as the natural basis for effective reciprocal relationship. The desire for reciprocity moved the observation of time and of tense into a new realm of agency for protohumans. Grooming generated an expectation of a learned future response of nurturing, caring touch in a relationship, one not driven by dominance or fight-or-flight survival risk. This set up a fresh interaction with time, a creative mental space where time connected to intention, to the inception of self-awareness, and to the projection of feeling and expectation onto another. As a protohuman focused on picking fleas, he or she aimed a small arrow of attention and intention at future grooming encounters and expected a return on investment. It was loose and detached from reactivity so as not to disrupt the peace of the present encounter. But it was enough to begin to clear a sacred interior space for contemplating the future, the self, and the other.

Sounds produced naturally during grooming—ahs of relief, squeaks of discomfort, and grunts of requests—would have become a kind of play across the I-Thou boundary in a relaxed environment of deep, loving attention. The meaning transcended survival signals. Vocal play within attuned energy fields held potential for subtlety and creativity in communication. The group members would need them when their fur was gone and language replaced grooming in holding the group together. But in the beginning, it gave them a field in which self-expression could begin to flower with playful musicality.

As our ancestors sensitized their awareness of the "other" during grooming, both sexes' capacity for nurturing would have grown in both observational skills and active responsiveness. Parental and communal care of the young could have become attuned with this new sensitivity, and that increased child survival rates and the ability to pass on skills. Parenting behavior learned in childhood and later imitated had potential to develop in complexity and innovation from the skills that grooming honed. That growth could have progressed at either incremental or exponential rates between generations. The primary group's level of sharing contained more possibility for growth than mother-to-child exposure alone.

Humans' creative capacity is very much based on hand sensitivity, dexterity, and coordination (of the eyes, ears, and hands) in the business of making music, art, tools, and writing. The flexible, creative neocortical circuits were patterned by and for our hands. It is an awesome blessing that our hands had a stress-free arena in which to pattern flexible networks of nerve connections in the brain that could one day produce an unlimited array of language and art. Survival patterns alone would have tended to generate more rigid memory storage and emotional reactivity.

The modern egoic self has an uncanny ability to filter out information from the senses, and to focus within itself, disconnected from primal sensory input. This can even happen in situations where it is dangerous and does not serve life (as in distracted driving). For me, this forcefully indicates that this capacity for consciousness was formed in a very relaxed, safe environment and not honed in immediate survival reactivity.

Naked, Ashamed, and Lost

We lost our fur. Language replaced grooming as the way we maintained group cohesion and identity. When and how this happened is a mystery. The group structure shifted, and a personal-space distance became part of human relationship patterns. This suggests to me that conscious awareness of some type of contagion was a major driver for that change. An increase in sweat glands and a concomitant decrease in hair follicles likely were factors in fur loss over time in equatorial climes, but the abandonment of grooming behavior, with its social and health benefits, suggests a traumatic cause.

A fear of contagion probably helped drive human dispersal over the globe. The search for a new, more nourishing place would have had a component of fear of disease and of contagion. Bands of humans entered and settled some very harsh frigid, arid, and swampy domains and learned to eke out an existence. Did they seek safety from a mysterious curse? Did they seek safety by isolating themselves from diseased populations? The group immune system rejected many benefits of the relaxed shared energy fields of grooming for fear of contagion. The sense of a separate self that was cultivated by and for the grooming community lost its grounding. The community members must have experienced fear of abandonment as a constant companion and equated it with fear of death. Connection through words and fear could bind the community, but could not bring grooming's physical, comforting energy to the insecure self. Shame as original sin, as a state of mind, became part of the human condition. We still struggle with that wound today in our attempts to secure and recover a positive self-image for ourselves and our offspring.

When evolution left us standing upright, we circled together for protection, turning to each other and learning more communal intimacy, the formative seeds of culture. The adaptable, creative, and refined nurturing skills that we developed through grooming expanded to include other species, both plant and animal, in the cultural expansion we named the Agri*cultur*eal Revolution. Living with herded species, such as sheep and goats, provided a rich, fertile environment for the opportunistic parasite populations of both species to adapt and thrive in shared company. The loss of fur may have been a very necessary adaptation to these increasing and adapting parasite infestations.

Infectious skin processes were readily visible, and the first human awareness of contagious infection could likely have happened with skin disease. Infection could be observed to move between close companions or grooming companions. When the community made the association and the signs were evident, the community likely shunned the infected one. This would have brought the birth of shame. As the infection progressed through generations, less fur may have become desirable for community and personal survival in the herding context. The nuclear group that shared touch would have shrunk to the family in many instances. Grooming decreased with loss of fur and increase of fear of contagion. Females had less choice about personal space in mating and nurturing processes. Males could choose more personal space and distance as a way to cope with infection. This may have influenced the differences in hair patterns between the sexes.

Amid mysterious threats to skin and hair, the poor neocortex—a group immune organ developed to manage fleas—had a huge new challenge. It had to redefine the group and its manners and structures to both accommodate life with other species and create safety in isolation practices to avoid contagious contact. This directly contradicted the old instinct to circle closer for protection. How to recreate the solidarity of the old group immune system without the closeness, energy, and intimacy of grooming? Without grooming, which naturally releases rage and fear hormones after conflict, reconciliation and forgiveness were and are much more difficult.

With the group as the primary survival unit, the group equated belonging with life itself. A consciousness grown by the group and essentially for the group had no reference or grounding for life outside the group. It was an empty chasm of terror. Shame was the terrible unbelonging,

To explore this further, consider the ancient biblical scriptures and how they resonate with feelings of shame. In the ancient memory of origins from the Middle East, the stories of both Adam and Eve and Noah in Genesis associate nakedness with intense shame.

"I was afraid, because I was naked; and I hid myself."[17]

"Noah was the first tiller of the soil. He planted a vineyard; and he drank of the wine, and became drunk, and lay uncovered in his tent. And Ham, the father of Canaan, saw the nakedness of his father, and told his two brothers outside. Then Shem and Japheth took a garment, laid it upon both their shoulders, and walked backward and covered the nakedness of their father; their faces were turned away, and they did not see their father's nakedness."[18]

Both these instances speak to a deep shame about nakedness. Did people originally learn shame about nakedness because they lost fur to disease? Was this a remnant of the memory of losing hair in a disease process that forced shunning? Fur loss may have been caused by parasitic skin disease. The use of clothing to cover diseased skin and avoid shunning could have hastened the loss of fur. Skin exposure gave high visibility to skin disease. Skin diseases likely gave groups a traumatic introduction to the terrible power of contagion. In some societies full coverage in robes may have been chosen to stabilize a frightened group. Any visible skin changes or differences would have produced deep fear after contagion had come into awareness. Clothing hid the furless body, which, if exposed, could reveal a skin condition, and it also prevented some spread of skin disease. Any visible skin irritation or condition, whether or not contagious, would trigger fear. Building boundaries about contagion is a continuing, long learning process. Better to cover up than to always live in fear of disease or shunning. It was better for society if everyone covered up, or else any irritated patch of skin could create fear and cause community relationships to crumble.

Shame over disease was transferred and associated with lack of clothing. Clothing gave humans a way to avoid and prevent shame. Imagine a communal group that fractured because it perceived that a skin disease was spreading through it. Many families would have split up, with parents having to decide whether to go into exile with a diseased child or to let the child die alone. Imagine the terror created when a child got poison ivy in a time before people could discernibly diagnose skin problems. We should not underestimate

---

17 Genesis 3:10 (Revised Standard Version).
18 Genesis 9:20–23 (Revised Standard Version).

the impact that contagious skin disease had on the disintegration of group cohesion. How much may these ancient memories of terrible, mysterious danger still influence our reactions to our own and others' skin?

We could interpret the biblical "knowledge of good and evil" as the terrible burden of having to define the group with language and law, instead of with the intimacy of shared energy fields. The tree could symbolize transcendence; safety sought in a higher, distanced perspective grew a new symbolic meaning in choices of good and evil. The sad new task for egoic consciousness was to redefine social relationship with safe distance, language, and law. The old grooming atmosphere had been intimate, safe, and nurturing. The fear of contagion left group life an encounter with dangerous strangers to control with words, laws, and strict manners. Intimacy was limited to the family. The neocortex faced huge demands to manage group health against threats of contagion, and the level of shame indicates just how traumatic it was—an "original sin" over which the individual had no control. Each affected individual had to accept that he or she did not "belong" any longer. For example, the disease of leprosy could claim a life in shame and shunning. There was no sure answer, no secure protection. All had to carry the insecurity. One can easily imagine a scenario where using clothing to both hide and protect the body from skin disease was a needed adaptation to preserve any social structure from terrible chaos.

A shepherding culture produced the Genesis scripture. Living with animals multiplies the complexity of disease processes within population densities. Contagion planted psychic wounds of unique intensity and nuance in each culture's group memory. Genesis 27[19] has an interesting reference to hair in the story of Esau and Jacob, which might reflect an ancient memory. In it, Esau is a hunter and Jacob a shepherd. Esau is his father's favorite and Jacob his mother's favorite. Esau is hairy and Jacob is smooth skinned. Jacob's mother covers his hands and neck with baby-goat fur in order to pass Jacob off as Esau to the blind father, Isaac. This story associates hairiness with masculinity and hunting in the character of Esau, and it associates Jacob's smooth skin with femininity and herding. The connections may be random, or they may have been very important in the ancient memory. By trickery, the herder receives the blessing in place of the hunter.

The Middle Eastern Judeo-Christian culture has shaped underlying

---

[19] Revised Standard Version.

social structures of the West. We carry its wisdom, and underneath our conscious choice, we also carry its wounds. Hearing the ancient stories from a herder's perspective suggests to me a neglected meaning—a deeply buried unconscious pain. Understanding the unique stresses of this shepherding culture can uncover misunderstood dynamics in the masculine–feminine and dominance–nurture balances within our modern community. Already deeply shaken by shame, an organized herding culture's identification and projection choices presented more unresolvable conflicts in the psyche. But resolution is now within our capacity. It is safe to make those conflicts conscious. It is safe to reclaim our wholeness.

CHAPTER 5

Self-Awareness

Self-awareness is a real enigma for humans. Before our ancestors grew a neocortex, we had a sensate selfhood with boundaries that functioned consistently so we experienced life as part of nature, with a knowledge of body and boundaries defined by sensation. Now, we have an added abstract sense of selfhood that seems to define our boundaries very differently. Our language shows this as an objectification of our parts as separate pieces. We say, "My leg hurts," as though our leg is a separate possession, instead of "I hurt in my leg"; or we say, "My mind is elsewhere." Our abstract self has rather indefinable boundaries in space and time, and it has often ambiguous connections to the sensate body at best. What we are in our own minds is a bit of a mystery. How did this happen?

In his book *The Inner Eye: Social Intelligence in Evolution*,[20] Nicholas Humphrey presents a truly enlightened argument that the primary evolutionary purpose of human consciousness is to look within and understand others in terms of self. Its primary purpose is not self-knowledge but self as a useful reference for identification and projection. Humphrey writes that "an 'inner eye' served one purpose before all: to allow our own ancestors to raise social life to a new level."[21] While I am not aware if

---

[20] Humphrey, Nicholas. *The Inner Eye: Social Intelligence in Evolution*. New York: Oxford University Press, 2002.

[21] Ibid., 11.

Humphrey made the connection to grooming, his insight would support the theory that an identification and projection dynamic likely sourced our human consciousness.

Another analogy or framework from which to observe the "inner eye" or egoic self is as part of a shared group immune system, developed by and for the group's survival purposes. Understanding its purpose can allow us to be present to its process with insight and compassion.

A primate's primary motivation to provide a good grooming experience for another did not start with wanting to please the other. It started with wanting the other's (initially the mother's) help to remove fleas. A social contract emerged as a way to feel better. The ultimate motivation for sensitive grooming was to better one's own personal experience. Over hours of grooming, primates slowly learned mutuality. The intent to identify and serve the other's wants first served the primary intent of receiving similar attention. They had relaxed time to feel the increased pleasure in the overlapping energy fields and to notice the other's behavior, smells, breathing, heartbeat, and other vibrations. How could one put meaning to these sensations that could recreate and improve grooming sessions? One could only guess meaning from one's own experience. "How would that feel to me?" A great skill honed in grooming was identification with the other and his or her feelings. Projecting that answer from the self onto the other would usually work. When it did not, our ancestors would learn a new boundary limit between self and other, such as differing levels of sensitivity or ticklishness. From within shared and synchronized energy fields, identification and projection skills had the potential to grow in subtlety and facility. The new circuitry growing in our ancestors' brains was birthed within a practice of presence, of skillful attention that would grow into the conscious practice of kindness.

Attunement to the other would have used abstract awareness of the self as its reference. It was an abstract reference because the question was not "What do I feel?" but "What would I feel if this were done to me?" An abstract self-concept would have been a byproduct of the effort to "know" the other. Self-knowledge was not the direct desire. The sensate self could provide sensory memory information, but its own wisdom and boundary domain stayed distinct from this new exploration. These new processes developed in support of group, not individual, survival, and only a limited integration is in the sensate self's best interests. Our abstract egoic self-concept grew as a secondary effect. It was and still is a reference component for a larger social consciousness, initially an immune system against parasites. Its immediate purpose was not to know the self but to know and control the other's reaction to the self within the group. This generated cohesion with the group. Thus, it was and is a very limited self-image, not nearly as well integrated with the sensate body as with the group social structure. Naming *ego* as a false self in our spiritual belief systems reflects the social and physical reality of its first purpose, which was to establish role and position in the community. The egoic self's development harshly veered away from focusing on self and other over a safe, intimate boundary space, to managing that focus with language in a complex space of law and an impersonal, institutionalized morality.

This fragile, egoic self's growth and strength was connected to a growth in time perception. By projecting beyond the immediate sensory boundaries, the desire of future reciprocity would have provided a framework where one could consider time abstractly. The abstract self could be projected into imagined time and space. With practice, this abstract self of referenced sensory memory could grow into a bigger concept with desire focused in imagined place and time. Imagination was a rich fruit of these projections. And imagination would be critical to support group survival beyond the death of grooming.

The primate group was the corporate body identified with survival. A well-constructed, abstracted *separate* selfhood would have no useful role for the group. The sensate selfhood was a primal, unconscious being that would not and could not safely integrate or surrender all of its power over the body into a fledgling, abstract construct of selfhood in service to the group. Originally, self-awareness meant identification and projection within social function. The first consciousness of this egoic self as a separate individual apart from the group likely came as a fear of separation from the group, a separation equated with death. This fear was not just about physical survival. Without the relationship system that produced the abstract image of self, the image could collapse.

This fragile egoic self was created to secure a future return on investment in a close community, and to uphold a bond in a group immune response to parasitic invasion. It had no existential ground outside of that relationship system. Its death was separation. When a creature first faced projecting that self-image into a future apart from the group, it could not. The image had no reality in any other realm. It fell apart. This was a literally unimaginable death for that self-image. Imagination and language would later span the distances in time and space and create the internal conversations that allowed that fragile egoic self to survive some separation, and to do it in a way that served community. This demonstrates the flexibility and plasticity in the neural networks that support consciousness. They can grow and transform. But fear of the egoic death of separation remains. It remains with us as a projection about physical death, a projection not based on any known truth.

Grooming as the primary group bond stopped in our ancestral line. We lost our fur. Body hair became a threat to our survival. We don't know how or why. Shame and fear of shame loom in our human psyche with great power. How do we account for that in our formative history? It is an interesting speculation to connect shame to the loss of fur. As early or protohumans with great nurturing skills learned to keep other species as part of their circle, perhaps the shared parasite population blossomed in some way that made fur a liability. However it happened, losing the grooming experience as part of the group structural definition left that frail ego consciousness, that embryonic self-awareness, in a frightful mess. How could the group preserve peace without the energy and hormonal reconciliation of grooming? How could humans justify this egoic self? How could humans feel part of a whole again? How could humans regulate relationships at a distance without shared energy fields and sympathetic, synchronized body rhythms? Life to this fragile egoic self, which had been born in connection, became populated by strangers. What terrible grief and fear! Despite our amazing adaptations of language and law, part of us has never recovered from floundering in that emptiness and primal self-doubt.

Exclusion from grooming left one feeling unworthy of a self and unworthy of life. The egoic self had to generate a new social order to sustain the group for its own survival. It had to leave the garden of sweet, relaxed refreshment and connection and make its way in a strange world. The ancient Genesis stories echo feelings of shame and loneliness, and the unrefined, opportunistic, raw potential to rise to the challenge of preserving community connections from a distance. The image of the tree echoes the role of transcendence, the power of the abstracted image, to recreate relationship at a safer distance through language and law. The depth of shame associated with nakedness in both Genesis stories, Adam and Eve and Noah, suggests that the protection that clothing afforded was not as much about the elements as about community life. It protected both against contagious, diseased skin and against the shame that could lead to ostracism when visible skin conditions suggested contagious disease. Clothing helped the community manage skin disease by both limiting physical contact and avoiding hysterical shunning reactions to any skin problem. It provided a barrier to shame in that it could prevent shunning. Clothing has also become a canvas that a fragile ego can use to project to others a new personal image and try to influence others' response to the self in many creative ways.

This text reflects my own identification and projection about my ancestors' experience. I put it out there for the reader's consideration in the hope that it might stimulate new connections to ancient memories—a primal resonance with loving presence as the source of who we are—and that it may open a space for healing ancient communal wounds within a safe remembering, calling home lost parts of our souls. Healing comes from recognizing the limits and purpose of our consciousness. If we try to use it to dominate and denigrate our sensate self as "less than," life loses its beauty and richness. Fear of death will dominate us. Consciousness has the flexibility to unify us within, to connect to our reptilian brain in love, and to hold all parts of our humanity in loving conversation.

As an interesting aside, could the compelling nature of the cultural phenomenon of texting be rooted in the memory of using thumbs in creating connection? Does it resonate in our circuits as a way to "keep in touch" that can bring more satisfaction than hearing a voice?

Can we heal the frightened, hate-filled voices in our psyches by cultivating loving presence to each other in safe groups? Can we honor the distanced judgment of law and language for their purpose of social organization and at the same time honor and practice the inherent belonging and the necessary power of touch for full human beingness? Do we have disease processes we can now manage, but about which we still carry old unconscious fears? How much is our fear of the stranger generated by a communal immune system for which skin appearance is a primary fear factor? Can synchronized energy fields induce deep relaxation and resculpt traumatized brain circuitry? There is much to make deliberately conscious about how we can influence the sympathetic and parasympathetic systems in human bodies through presence and synchronization of energy fields. This influence is not new.

We are attuned to it in body. Everyone has seen, if not experienced, it in crowds at sporting events (home-field advantage), at religious services, and at hate rallies. Grade schools could teach all that we can consciously know of these dynamics as skills for participating in a peaceful community. For consciousness to grow, it must recognize its true self as social sustainer— how to breathe as one while enjoying and loving the individual's unique boundaries.

Our humanness was born in a field of loving, relaxed connection. There, we learned the nurture that could support creative boundary and relationship experiments. We learned to modulate dominance instincts and fear reactions so that life could evolve and a huge, dense population of diverse talent could serve it—in so many new ways as to triple life expectancy. As numbers increase, so do the intensity and complexity of shared fields. What can we remember, recreate, and expand from our seminal experience that can serve us now? How can we consciously serve the communal field with our energy so we create the most happiness or the most fulfilling human experience?

Can we unlearn fear of death by appreciating the role of our egoic self as a protective, communal immune system incapable of being a real self? Can we connect that ego with all its limitations in an exuberant union with our sensate body and, through our sensate body, know our union with all that is?

There are an infinite number of questions to ask of the power of love (gravity), and each has many answers.

CHAPTER 6

Herding

Let's consider our ancestral experience of introducing animals into the human family circle as a way to optimize access to meat, skins, milk, and fiber, without the dangers of hunting. Herding, like hunting, was mostly seen as part of the masculine domain. Males remained responsible for slaughter. But the two experiences—herding and hunting—were not comparable beyond the fact that they both yielded meat. Hunting provided an attuned connection to nature and hormonal support for the slaughter. Slaughtering a nurtured creature was an entirely different experience.

Herding's choices persist as a vital part of human identity. In all endeavors, we learn by identification and projection, whether with the worthy prey or with the slaughtered lamb. In the service of physical prosperity, herding proved so successful that to this day, we have never consciously evaluated or openly negotiated its cost to the social contract, to human culture, and to our souls. Strong voices in our society advocate for compassionate treatment of animals. Some choose vegetarianism to resolve the felt conflicts. Attitudes and feelings about cultivated species differ by species and culture. These relationships are not only trans-species but transpersonal. These interspecies relationships have been rich and rewarding. But they have also wounded our souls, as the violence inherent to these relationships has subconscious, layered, subtle, and fierce manifestations throughout human cultures. As we explore these wounds, I would suggest that judging herding (or hunting, or the differences between the two) moralistically will be counterproductive to self-discovery and healing. Only by being fully present for all the dimensions of our experience as herders can we renegotiate the herders' choices with a mature, conscious acceptance and reclaim our wholeness.

Our relationships with herded species rely on our cultivated nurturing capacities that emanate from our projection and identification skills. All herded species are familiar to us in that they live in groups with dominance structures like our own. That allowed us to know and understand them by identification and projection. It would be hard to distinguish whether they learned to be our herd or we learned to be part of their herd. These relationships inherently affect our self-image, for those projections inevitably reflect their violence back onto relationships within our species. They are a subconscious and unacknowledged price of herding. We have waited long enough to actually examine and reform these dynamics in a way that feeds our souls and bodies.

All the skills occasioned by grooming lent strong creative power to the human capacity to nurture. A marvelous repertoire of observational and responsive skills flourishes in both sexes. Humans accomplished the immense challenge of regrouping after the loss of grooming's social glue—reshaping all that shared energy in a consciously created communal structure, with its cohesiveness bound in language and law—in a miraculous expansion of nurture into the artfulness of culture. But it also entailed losing a layer of social intimacy to a distancing personal space. On account of both learnings—the hole and the bridge—that creative flexibility was able to encompass other species. Out of the breadth and depth of these new skills came agriculture. Humans nurtured other species, plant and animal. Having to grow a human culture broadened the potential for other powers of cultivation across species gaps.

The mental process was still identification and projection. It had big potential for serious errors in expanding its uses beyond the human realm. In the words of Richard Feynman, "How do we get new ideas? That you do by analogy, mostly, and in working with analogy you often make very great errors."[22] *Analogy* means projecting what you perceive from an old experience onto a new experience, another term for *identification* and *projection*. Using the human experience to understand and to act in cultivation of another animal species imparts new dimension, color, conflict, and value back onto

---

[22] Feynman, Richard. *The Meaning of It All*. New York: Perseus, 1998.

the self through the identification process. For example, controlling a herd of sheep requires recognition of the dominance workings within that herd. This is available through identification and projection skills. The herder experiences human dominance behavior that allows him to see something like it at work in the flock and to advantageously use it to control the flock. He will also learn something from relating to the flock that will reflect back onto his human relationships. And any new relationship is full of wonder and attuned energy. He can feel love and divinity at work.

Anthropologically, plant cultivation skills are usually defined as feminine, extensions of the female food-gathering role. Yet, they were not confined to female community members. Agriculture was a tribal activity that emerged within the whole community as an expression of refined feminine energy. The feminine nurturing capacity of all humans, male and female, advanced these skills, and in the Neolithic Age, the divine feminine was the focus of worship. Goddess images both contained and inspired the unfolding gift of nurturance.

Encounters with the divine are most vivid and most needed at the growing edge of civilization, as support for stepping into the unknown. The "validity" of these experiences is not really a valid question. We are to enjoy, not judge, the dynamics of how creative mystery manifests. Myth allows us to encounter mystery in community.

The neural circuitry that enabled these steps into myriad interspecies relationships would have been quickly overwhelmed without the capacity for group memory, and a verbally shared cultural repository for the ever-expanding accumulation of skill and information. Complex learning became institutionalized as a community survival resource. It consumed a large expenditure of community investment and personal life span, requiring both longer childhood training and tribal roles devoted to maintaining the stories. The neural plasticity of that initial group immune system that fleas sparked was so creatively adaptable! But the unmet challenge was how to restore and maintain peace without the daily, nurturing shared energy fields of grooming. Without grooming's relief, stress also became institutionalized in human culture and agriculture. Law and punishment replaced the reconciliation processes of grooming. The reassuring *belonging* felt in communal grooming transformed into a desire for the frequently elusive sense of worthiness.

The agricultural revolution is often viewed as the expression of human dominance over other species, especially in herding. But in truth, the key to success was a finely tuned feminine nurturing skill. Relationships with other species depended on our capacity to strongly identify with herded species' needs and welfare. This still shows up in deeply personal language, such as *animal husbandry*. The boundaries between species were and are held in human consciousness in a storm of crosswinds, tossed and torn in conflict between unity and separateness, nurture and dominance, and masculine and feminine. This storm has raged long enough without full conscious engagement. In some arenas, dominance behavior may look like a clear "winner," but the human soul frequently hides in the rubble of its own fear, afraid to come out and claim its truth. I propose that herding conflicts became embodied in the structure of our split brain. The neurological circuits for nurture and for dominance learned to hide from each other. From one perspective, they learned to protect each other and stay out of each other's space.

Our first significant interspecies relationship (besides with parasites) was with wolves as they evolved under our direction into dogs. It was one of mutual cooperation between two hunting species that understood and practiced dominance and nurture in similar ways. In this mutually beneficial working relationship, both species targeted other species for shared meals and mostly refrained from eating each other. After man's best friend, sheep[23] and goats were the next most widely domesticated species. They kept close groups with a dominant leader and thus were easy to control, a task well within the capacity of our identification and projection skills. Adaptable and docile, they would breed in captivity, and in many ways, we had a mutually beneficial relationship. Sheep are easy prey, and the herd thrives under human protection. Human nurturing skills provide access to food and water and help with birthing, disease, injury, and care of the young.

Early shepherds cared for sheep as they did their families, sharing water and shelter with constant vigilance. Caves in the Negev Desert have revealed some of the earliest evidence of domestic herding. Preserved dung showing that both shepherds and their flocks of sheep and goats sheltered themselves

---

[23] Clutton-Brock, Juliet. *A Natural History of Domesticated Animals*. Austin: University of Texas Press, 1987.

in caves has been carbon-dated as far back as 5000 BC.[24] While this is the first evidence, a few animals likely accompanied families thousands of years before this role of shepherd emerged as a main survival strategy. The shepherd continuously kept lambs, with all their playfulness and exuberance, under his protective gaze. In return, the herd provided high-quality meat, fiber, milk, and hides. We can see the trade-offs as win-wins from the quality-of-life perspective, if just simplistically quantified. But the herding relationship posed a more complex emotional challenge.

For the shepherd, slaughtering demanded that compartmentalization and dissociation be actively strengthened as mental and emotional skills. The hunters' attunement to nature and unity was not available to support the herders' experience of slaughter. The shepherd needed to shut down his nurturing side when it came time to kill. He had to split from any previously felt unity consciousness, from any connection to the animal's essence, and from his nurturing self that "knew" the animal. It would be important for a young man growing into the shepherding role to "not be a woman" at slaughter time. The stronger his feminine drive to nurture (which would make a more successful shepherd), the more conflicted he would feel about the slaughter. He would have to stuff down and deny the feminine aspects of his personality—a terrible internalized conflict of the sexes—leaving the feminine as a force to be used and then to be conquered. I am suggesting that this unresolved challenge persists in the subconscious of both sexes, in structural adaptations in our individual brains, and in our shared community consciousness. My own experience of the difficulty of staying fully present to both the anticipation and the execution of sheep slaughtering supports my view.

Given that we share more than 90 percent of our DNA with other animals, I don't judge the mental and emotional conflicts that come with human identification and projection with animals as an artifact of immaturity. The boundaries between species are difficult, murky, and shifting positions with which we have always struggled and likely always will. The compartmentalization that we developed to manage the conflict between

---

[24] Rosen, Steven A., Arkady B. Savinetsky, Yosef Plakht, Nina Kisseleva, Bulat F. Khassanov, Andrey M. Pereladov, and Mordecai Haiman. "Dung in the Desert: Preliminary Results of the Negev Holocene Ecology Project," *Current Anthropology* 46, no. 2 (2005): 317–327.

nurture instincts and dominance instincts in our relationship to animals has projected itself back onto the human species' social consciousness. This compartmentalizing has proved very useful to mental logic and scientific analysis for narrow problem solving, and at the same time has opened a self-destructive path, with its bypass of holistic perspective—for example, in deciding to put pesticides in our crops and antibiotics in our meat. During exponential growth in response to demands for change and adaptation, balance can only be maintained through movement. Wounds and losses get buried in the drive forward. As in our personal childhood, so in our evolutionary childhood growth proceeds apace, ready or not. At the right time, wisdom dictates we revisit and heal old wounds.

The evolutionary shift from hunter to herder was a complex and warping event for the psyche. Let's try to fathom its impact with some projection and identification. Imagine an early human male taking his son on a foray with a hunting party. The son would get an intense lesson in attunement. It would include attunement to the hunting group's energy and its leadership structure and communication style; attunement to the prey's movements and habits, sensory capacities, smells and signs, and defensive strategies; and attunement to weather, wind, water, plants, tracks, shadows, and sounds. The party could ignore no sensory input, no movement, no environmental change, and no element of personal presence.

This intense attunement to all in the present moment creates a wondrous high, or unity of creation, tribe, and self, and it has an intense hormonal imprint. The predator honors and respects its prey by knowing its essence, power, and place in the scheme of life. The predator–prey relationship has a deep and powerful spiritual basis in unity consciousness. The hunt's success depends on a predator's respect for the prey—how well the predator truly sees, knows, and appreciates the prey in its natural environment. Knowing and celebrating the prey in its separateness precedes recalling it into unity as food. This full expansion of awareness and intense connection to all of nature is both a cultivated skill and a spiritual gift for the hunter.

Fresh challenges in a hunt created an appreciation for each individual creature's uniqueness. Hunters who were attuned to nature and the hunted would have experienced a powerful connection as part of their success, and each experience would be unique. Thus, for a young boy to enter the hunters' ranks was a momentous passage. Celebration, gratitude, and spiritual connection were all components of the experience, along with excitement and hormonal highs. The experience built community, communication, discipline, and intuition. Unity consciousness was, in fact, a spiritual space inherent to daily survival in the hunt.

Now, contrast that experience with that of a shepherd who teaches his son to harvest meat from the herd. That experience would include little excitement or anticipation beyond dread. The animal is also well studied and known, but known as a creature the family nurtures and cares for, not as challenging prey. In fact, the family has protected it from being prey to other creatures, and its role as meat is not separate and does not fit the primal predator–prey relationship. There is no call to unity except that felt as grief. There is no intense attunement to the tribe or nature that provides hormonal support. The tribe may honor the creature with gratitude for its flesh. Harvesting meat includes important lessons to learn: honing a very keen edge and knowing exactly where to cut the neck artery to let the animal quickly bleed out with minimum pain. People will often mourn for the animal's essence, for they first experience its essence as part of the nurtured group.

The lesson teaches compartmentalization in distancing from emotion and in facing the psyche's trade-offs and pain with hard resolve. It is a lonely, conflicted, often alienating encounter with a divided self. This has a deep shadow, disconnecting parts of the inner soul and sending them away from the table. The shepherd likely would have anticipated the lamb's birth—perhaps even aided in its birthing and certainly celebrated its birth. At every stage of the lamb's development, the herder oversaw and perhaps supplemented the feeding and care of the lamb by the ewe. The lamb's playfulness and exuberance likely brought the herder joy as he diligently observed its care and protection. The herder's investment in care and nurture—with all its natural feminine hormonal and emotional components—would culminate in grief, guilt, and pain when he had to harvest that lamb's meat. Without the experiential and hormonal rewards of a successful hunt, slaughtering the grown lamb was a hard and hardening task. He had to hone a vital new skill for disattunement.

The father–son relationship was cruelly altered. The stronger a man or woman's feminine drive to nurture, the more conflicted the slaughter made him or her feel. Whereas hunting can help fathers and sons bond, the lesson of slaughtering nurtured animals is hard on the herder's children, and especially hard on the father–son relationship. The shared heart space can become a dark, divided hole. Instead of seeing the slaughter as an opportunity for expanded awareness about death within unity consciousness, the children were taught to ignore their emotions and shut down feelings. The slaughter suddenly betrayed the knowing of the animal that the herding relationship fostered. Thus, children learned that death is an onerous task, a dark hole of dissociation. The meat may have fueled a celebration, but the act of killing itself held no glory, no honor, and no bonding. Thus was bred a shadowy, internal struggle with death, held in a separate dark place in the mind without the context of unity consciousness. This disconnection was defined as "being a man" and projected easily to other parts of our human self-image. But it differed greatly from the hunter's identification with the man who brought home the meat.

The herding story that unfolded in the Middle East is perhaps the most significant shaping force for Western culture, in part because the Old Testament recorded the experience and carefully maintained and embraced it as a cultural basis. The Old Testament speaks the glorious benefits as well as the intense conflict and pain inherent in the shepherd's choice with a sacred power and solemnity. It carefully recounts them, but the usual interpretation directly bends away from the herding experience and usually asks other questions. Images of divine power enforce personal distance from the herding choices. There is a great gift in recording experiences forced deep beneath the surface, even though current interpretation is directed at dissociation. The scriptural writings are a great resource that quite directly reveals the depths of conflict if we are ready to see them, so I will use them to help bring the wonder and the wounding into a compassionate light.

No better expression of the early herder's conflicted internal life exists than the story of Abraham's near murder of his son Isaac, often called the trial of Abraham (Genesis 22). In this story, Abraham hears God ask him to offer his son Isaac as a blood sacrifice. At the last minute, a divine reprieve occurs, and a ram is offered instead. The story is usually interpreted as God's test of Abraham's obedience. Perhaps that diverts a bit from a deeper meaning.

In truth, Abraham would gain great prosperity as a reward for his willingness to sacrifice his son. By learning to separate himself from his nurturing side and from his parental love, and do this on demand, he could achieve wealth and power as patriarch. This capacity to compartmentalize and conquer feelings about nurture—to project the unresolvable conflict onto God—enabled lucrative herding practices. It still does. And imagine the effect on the father–son relationship. Before Abraham heard the reprieve, "he bound his son Isaac and put him on the altar on top of the wood. Abraham stretched out his hand and seized the knife to kill his son."[25] Even though a reprieve occurred, Isaac saw his father as his killer in the name of God.

The dark complexities of this story spiral even deeper. To optimize herd size, it is necessary to cull most young male lambs. Ewes and lambs are manageable, but rams are dangerous, as their name suggests. When not culled of most adult males, a large herd would become uncontrollable and generate broken bones and injuries similar to hunting injuries. Castration delays maturation and aggression so that shepherds could harvest young rams over a slightly longer time and put more meat on their bones prior to slaughter. Allowing rams to overtake a herd would lead to a mismanagement of resources. Fertile ewes must make up the bulk of a prosperous herd in order to support a large tribe. Only a few well-chosen rams are needed to service the ewes. One ram can breed thirty to seventy-five ewes. So most male lambs would have to be culled early on in a large herd.

On one level, this grew out of a simple economic necessity. However, when we place it in the holistic picture of the nurturing (identification and projection) relationship between the shepherd and the sheep, it shows a crippling emotional conundrum. Shepherds no longer slaughtered male lambs to put supper on the table. No, slaughtering took on a new purpose: the accumulation of stored wealth. Shepherds sacrificed young male sheep for prosperity's sake. And great blessings ensued. The herder patriarch could maintain his wealth and his tribal leadership into old age. Thus, God must desire this sacrifice of young rams. In the Bible, in response to Abraham's obedience, God does not just promise him that he will not go hungry. He says, "I will shower blessings on you, I will make your descendants as many as the stars of heaven and the grains of sand on the seashore. Your descendants shall gain possession of the gates of their enemies. All the nations of the earth shall less themselves by your descendants, as a reward for your obedience."[26] Here is the original prosperity gospel. I have always marveled at the opportunism

---

[25] Genesis 22:9–10 (The Jerusalem Bible).

[26] Genesis 22:17–18 (The Jerusalem Bible).

that many biblical stories include. Equating success with God's favor can sanctify violence.

But who was this God, and how did the herding community envision him? Human consciousness, built on identification and projection, needs a God that will hold and manage conflict for us, a God onto whom we can project the painfully unresolvable. The demand on masculinity was to learn to split from the feminine at will. The interests of masculine dominance needed to override the nurture instinct. A uniquely male God was in order. The skills of both sexes—of dominance and of nurture—were both necessary for herding prosperity, but a separation happened. The two had to run in parallel circuits, which could interpenetrate less and less. They could not be held at the same time when the interests of each met in such emotional conflict. Polarization occurred in the mind—when in the masculine dominance mode, the feminine was shut out. Each mode grew its own neural circuitry with defined internal boundaries. This split was a violent internal act, and that violence projected into the social contract. Social life and brain structure reflected the split (now brilliantly reflected in the current U.S. political-party system).

One biblical passage really demonstrates the power of the herder's identification with sheep and the depth of the mental split: the story the prophet Nathan tells to King David in the twelfth chapter of Samuel 2. Nathan tells the story to make King David aware of the serious nature of his errors in coupling with Bathsheba and then arranging for her husband's death on the battlefield. The nature and effectiveness of Nathan's story and David's response to the story clearly show the intensity of the culture's nurturing love toward sheep. It shows how the identification and projection process remains the same between and within species.

Here is Nathan's story: "In the same town were two men, one rich and the other poor. The rich man had flocks and herds in great abundance; the poor man had nothing but a ewe lamb, one only, a small one he had bought. It was like a daughter to him. This he fed, and it grew up with him and his children, eating his bread, drinking from his cup, sleeping on his breast; it was like a daughter to him. When there came a traveler to stay, the rich man refused to take one of his own flock or herd to provide for the wayfarer who had come to him. Instead he took the poor man's lamb and prepared it for his guest."[27]

---

[27] 2 Samuel 12:2–4 (The Jerusalem Bible).

David's response, "this man who did this deserves to die,"[28] shows the depth of the nurturing connection in the herding relationship. Nathan then turns David's response back at David to rebuke his behavior. For me, the most fascinating information in this story is in the power of identifying with the sheep, with the ewe lamb. David feels the ewe's irreplaceability very deeply, as Nathan knew he would. Nathan did not highlight that David had effectively murdered Bathsheba's husband. He stayed carefully within the feminine nurturance domain to get David's attention, and he used a sheep to do that. Once David had impregnated Bathsheba, someone was going to die—either Bathsheba and her fetus at her husband's hand, or the husband by David's manipulation. The male dominance story had no possible good ending. Nathan stayed out of that story. If he had triggered those dominance circuits, it is unlikely David would have heard the pain and injustice that resulted from his behavior. The story clearly demonstrates the split in the psyche between the dominance and nurturance circuitry and how the separation can be manipulated.

By necessity, the herder must be both the predator and the nurturer *at different times*. Masculine and feminine capacities cooperated and collided in shepherding behavior with grave consequences for the human psyche. Humans acted out their old instinct toward infanticide to protect a genetic line on another species. The taboo loosened as it entered awareness in another form that humans accepted. It is interesting that infanticide begins both the story of the Exodus and that of the birth of Christ—the biggest transition times in the biblical story—echoing Abraham and Isaac.

A herd's size defined the tribal boundaries of who could trade and distribute food, wool, and hide. Herd size determined family size, the number of wives, and who was included in the extended family. The herding social structure made it possible to extend power in linear time, include issues of inheritance and lineage, and have influence and power from beyond the grave. Heady stuff! If a man could rule into old age, why not see how far he could extend his power? The Bible's recounting of the patriarchs' longevity celebrates longevity as an incredulous new possibility—the extension of the tribal chief's rule into old age. For the hunter/chief, life expectancy usually maxed out for his role, if not his physical life, at about age thirty-five. But a good herder could maintain his place as leader into old age.

---

[28] 2 Samuel 12:5 (The Jerusalem Bible).

No price was too high. The price became culling, devaluing the lives of male lambs, which complicated the human psyche in a distressing way, where all the shadows danced in identification and projection. The hunter internalized devaluing male lambs, and the herder's identification with the animal projected back onto human society. A man could best maintain his power and property into old age by investing his eldest son in protecting the father's interests as his own. One son was "chosen" as inheritor and the others devalued. Another shadowed reflection of the herder's choices projected onto social life when slavery and male castration became part of the human community's "natural" fabric of life. These practices could fit within a projected profile of those not chosen, those held in a place of nothingness in the group awareness, considered less than human and animals to exploit. Herders did not consciously or directly hold their internal conflicts about slaughter in their awareness—that was too difficult. They managed these conflicts with compartmentalization. But the awareness seeped beneath the surface of consciousness, generating symbols, new spiritual interpretations of divine order, and cold, human relationships to match.

Weather shifts in the Middle East came to better support nomadic shepherds than farmers. People abandoned feminine earth goddesses because they could not prevent drought and famine. A dissociated feeling of distrust toward the betraying feminine was reinforced by the nurturing of male lambs for slaughter. Betrayal by the feminine became iconic in Eve. An angry, jealous male God made his presence known to a chosen people. Religious "sacrifice" became a spiritual justification, or an emotional shield, for culling young rams from herds. The choosing of rams—those deemed best to keep for seeding the herd—became part of a painful template for a projected human masculine identity. With the internalization of culling as a subconscious identification, the dominance instinct saw itself in a life-and-death situation. Only the few best lambs were allowed to breed, and the rest were worthy only of death. The opposite of dominance, of being chosen, was not submission in the herding projection. It was death, or sacrifice. Can one trace the roots of the cold desperation of white privilege in Western culture back to the shadows of herding choices?

This terrorizing identification had the power to curdle the father–son bond. The split in consciousness left a cold emptiness and an impossible double message. Inherent in shepherding, devaluing the masculine, except for a few elite, echoed through the dominance circuitry of human males in fearful identification. Human males could not realistically satisfy their need to feel chosen. Every year, a herd underwent a new choosing and repeated slaughter. Worthiness for leadership became confounded with worthiness for life. People could and would experience being male as being under constant mortal challenge. Violence and betrayal were natural outcomes of this—attempts to bring the internal conflict to the surface, where people could face it by acting it out. To this day, these conflicts play out in violence, with the sources still buried in religious interpretation. That we remain trapped in these cycles of violence without resolution suggests to me that this old subconscious wound may control us today.

The Bible as the story of man's relationship to God—to a higher creative self—tells us much more about the human journey than about God. To approach scripture looking for this insight into ourselves does not deny God. It explores a loving relationship to creativity, an affirmation that God is creativity and love supporting our journey. The recorded human encounter with the divine reveals the growing edge of human experience. Humans had to put unity consciousness aside to herd. Dissociation was necessary. So was it best to have one God for a "chosen" people? One God within whom unity could be held—but at a distance? A God that was a disembodied voice? A God that lived in a box (the Ark of the Covenant)? A God that kindly held the conflicted human relationship with unity for his people, until they were ready to reclaim their wholeness? A God that willingly became the focus of their fear as they struggled with a crueler identity than they were equipped to experience? A God that was the God they needed in the moment, not a perfect ideal but a presence that stayed with them on any terms?

Let's look at the story of Cain and Abel as an example of the herding life's emotional cost. Cain was a farmer who fared badly with his crops while Abel, a shepherd, fared well with his herd. The climate was changing in a way that favored herding over crop cultivation. But Cain saw the cause as divine disfavor and God's preference for Abel's sacrifices. So the story goes that Cain killed his brother Abel. With Abel's herd of sheep and goats in tow, Cain assumed the nomadic life with great reluctance and regret. Even without the judgment of *murderer,* he lived his new life in exile from the land he loved, and it was born from a terrible feeling of unworthiness. His first love, his desired relationship to the nurturing earth, had betrayed him. Killing as slaughter was a necessary part of his new life. In the story, God allows Cain to live with all his internal conflict, granting him protection from vengeance. Alienated from the divine feminine, Cain perceives himself subject to a God of harsh judgment.

This story has a deeper meaning than just a story about murder. The psychological adaptations to herding increased tendencies toward violence between men. But people should also see the story as an expression of the painful internal experience of the reluctant nomadic herder—a result of a necessary choice that would haunt him and leave him in exile from his original self. Cain killed off part of himself to become a herder. The violence of cold slaughter required shutting down the nurturing parts of the self, and it deepened his alienation from the feminine. A perception of the feminine as betrayer helped fortify the psychic split between masculine and feminine, and justify the distance necessary to handle the slaughtering task. A reluctant resignation to the herder's life may have needed misogyny at that stage of human maturity. All humans have both testosterone and estrogen in their makeup. All have both dominance and nurture instincts. The balances in individuals and in communities vary. Both sexes adapted to the herding conflicts they both felt, with both carrying the cultural beliefs about sexual identity.

Zechariah 11 features another scriptural passage that expresses the dark conflicts that the culling practice raises in the human psyche: "This is how Yahweh spoke to me: 'Pasture the sheep bred for slaughter, whose buyers kill them and go unpunished, whose sellers say of them, '"Blessed be Yahweh; now I am rich!" and their shepherds handle them without kindness. For no longer am I going to show kindness to the inhabitants of the world—it is Yahweh who speaks. But instead I mean to hand over every man to the next and to his king. They shall devastate the world and I will not deliver them from their hands.'"[29]

In the human psyche, the same advancements that extended male leaders' life expectancy to a previously unimagined degree inherently betrayed and devalued the divine masculine within unity consciousness. A heightened worry about worthiness crippled masculine identity. An endless flow of double messages and blood sacrifice would maintain the split within the "chosen" self. Nurture, the divine feminine, could not be trusted in her

---

[29] Zechariah 11:4–6 (The Jerusalem Bible).

duplicitousness because she nurtured for slaughter. Human community prospered from herding; herding extended life and social organization with adroit flexibility. This tore human consciousness of life as a unitive, attuned experience at the core—again.

CHAPTER 7

Redemption

The experience of unity consciousness brings a felt sense of belonging and trust, sensory delight in being part of creation, passion for life in warm blood and powerful heartbeat, and surrender into the shared web of life energy. Unity is the sacred beingness our bodies know throughout life, regardless of what fearful domains our minds create; each life is a wonder of persistent genetic memory of how to live in a magically coordinated dance of elements and energies. This is divine presence as mystery. The face or voice of God is a projection of that presence, as it can most lovingly meet human creative needs. It has truth in it—the truth of the field of love holding and nurturing the limits of our identification and projection processes as they expand. Judging our adaptations and projections in hindsight as wrong denies them their beauty and power within their time and place. The great truth is in the constancy of loving support, as it takes the form we can most readily accept at each stage of our evolution.

The essential structure of our minds was birthed in the womb of the grooming experience. The haunting loss of the intimacy of regularly shared energy fields, with their inherent communal belonging, left an existential hole. This communal immune system struggled mightily to maintain the group connection. Law and punishment, words, and retribution were the new means of control. But in this new structure, everyone was exiled from the internal sense of belonging. While it was critical to maintain that sense of belonging for children, effective socialization required that the child be disabused of any sense of entitlement. Parents had to teach rules, discipline, and strict conformity to social governance and convention before they could safely release children into the alienation of the wider community. The longing for acceptance and security became identified as something to outgrow. But in truth, it is inherent to our brain structure and will always persist. Without it, our brains function incrementally, not holistically. And when fear and stress fortify the demand to serve the group more than love does, then joy is elusive.

Language brought powerful creative gifts to essence, which continue to expand. Words filled the emptiness of personal space with enough energy to keep it open and resonating, even as it shook with the fear of judgment. But the hole of longing for the simple being of grooming remains. We can fill and heal it. This possibility is the promise of redemption that biblical texts heralded. Trust in life demanded faith in that promise. Today, we can choose to be together in simple, close presence, consciously tapping the nurturing, healing potential of touch while also maintaining safety from disease. We can create moments for vacating judgment when we can rest and renew in essential connection. We have that available to us—not as transcendent, advanced spiritual potential for a few, but as basic mental, emotional, egoic hygiene that all can learn in childhood.

Divided Presence

After that little venture into radical hope, let's go back to how our Middle Eastern ancestors sought to heal the psychic violence of their herding experience. The longing for lost unity consciousness and attunement attempted to craft a new frame of reference for itself. The herder's egoic consciousness needed distance, an illusion of separation where he could do what he needed to do in the culling, but then return to a place of connection. Connection to unity needed its own space. With no interior resolution, the herder needed a projection to justify his action and to help carry his emotional split with himself.

How did monotheism offer some resolution or relief? People projected one male God in whom they proclaimed and idealized unity, whom they could experience as a disembodied voice, and whose presence could be contained in an ark or temple. This helped sustain them in a place of some comfort and hope. The projection of the single male deity echoed and justified the long-term, dominant clan leader's experience. Sacrificing the male sheep in the temple became a way of translating that experience into a statement of connection to unity, projecting the necessity as divine directive.

In their relationship to the divine, the Israelites saw themselves as chosen, echoing the deepened identity threat for the masculine dominance instinct. The relationship became one of petition rather than one of felt unity, of reaching for rather than living within. This covenantal relationship sought to connect to unity by means of words and spoken agreements. A word-based relationship could establish distance from and also build a bridge to the attuned, ecstatic presence to life. This is a much more difficult path for achieving a restorative, loving connection. A mental commitment to unity often substituted for the relationship's felt experience. A detachment from self, or a disembodied witness's voice, expressed the projection and identification that had lost their grounding in touch and shared energy fields. It appeared that unity consciousness had been taken hostage in human awareness by a powerful, angry male spirit—masculine power seeking elusive healing and trust in itself with a covenant that resembled the relationship between herder and herd. Being chosen distances one from unity, with an insecure, tenuous hold on the sense of belonging. In judgment, one loses the comfortable reassurance of being inherently part of creation.

The Herder's Wound Embodied

When people find a wound too painful to live with, they often project it onto the divine. I have heard people describe morphine as separating them from their pain. If religion is the "opiate of the people," it is a gift to treasure until healing comes. Let's now look at the Christ story as it expresses the herding wounds.

- The child is born in a manger with the livestock. That image is one of the most powerful in Christianity. It is spoken of as a "humble" beginning, demonstrating that the lowliest can identify with and participate in the story. But perhaps it holds in symbol, at a distance, the desire for an integrated relationship with the animals we keep to serve us.

- The first to be informed of his birth are shepherds. Angels present him as a source of great joy, a Savior. He comes first to heal the shepherds.
- At the Last Supper, the transformation of eating and being eaten is consecrated with the words "Take, eat; this is my body."[30]
- The Son of Man dies hanging from a cross like a butchered animal. He is the Son sacrificed, the Abraham and Isaac story retold with a crueler ending.

Is this the healing resolution, the redemption of the herder's pain? Is it a more vivid symbolic, sacred compartment for the cruel wound of separation? Is it both? The Christ story has had profound effects on civilization. The awakening seems inexhaustible. So, perhaps it is both.

The Last Supper's symbolism carries meaning that spans the basic hospitality of eating together, a reenactment of the sacrifice of the Son, and the divine immanent presence. In relation to herding wounds, the Communion Supper, the body, and the blood can be seen as a recollection and a sacred remembrance of the first ground of unity in nature: that of eating and being eaten. All eating is a sacred transformation of energy from one being into another. Our primal, reptilian selves understand that. Love can minimize the suffering in our consciousness by creating boundaries around this truth. Can we work out and reconcile relationships of eating and being eaten in ways that truly minimize suffering? The reptilian parts of ourselves hold survival energy that says yes to consuming and being consumed. That is a sacred yes. By that affirmation, they also hold the essence of forgiveness. In the deepest levels of unity consciousness, there is no other. To remember the unity with all that is makes forgiveness a nonissue. Your being is for giving— for transformation.

That the boundaries we create, those that are subject to human choice and control, separate us from unity is a psychic wound—a wound created in our consciousness. We live and die as earthlings, our energy always part of the earth's energy. Only within the frame of reference of our egoic consciousness can we be separated from the wholeness that gives us happiness and peace— from the parts of ourselves that feel excluded from the table and from each other. Suffering results from choosing a reality construct that is separate

---

[30] Matthew 26:26 (New Revised Standard Version).

from what is. What if we could treasure and honor separateness and unity equally? Can we minimize suffering in the name of separateness? Can we minimize suffering in the name of oneness? This balance will forever evade us. The balance can never hold or be held in some image of perfection. Free-flowing forgiveness is inherent in the attempt. Forgiveness means saying *yes* to life. Can we exercise compassion within the realities of life that frighten us, staying present to the whole as we care for the parts?

The human mind of the frontal brain is an organ formed and structured for the group—for relationship. Its function now depends on words rather than touch—on active conversations between creatures and conversations that are projected only internally. A healthy ego depends on healthy conversations. Because a group-bonding process based on law and punishment replaced one based on reconciliation, shame, fear, guilt, and unworthiness can intrude onto the psyche from many parts of communal chattering. Shame and fear were and are cultivated and used freely to cripple, contain, and control. Language has been refined to precisely compartmentalize meaning for law and science, rather than to support loving connection, leaving it a poor tool for connections of the heart. The heart hears connection in embodiment, the rhythms of breath and blood. To heal the primal wound from loss of grooming, "The Word Became Flesh."[31]

The Christ figure's loving and healthy masculine presence in the group consciousness was a great and much-needed gift. People accepted him as an intimate, internal companion—one with whom they could revisit the practices of forgiveness, unconditional love, inherent worthiness, soul healing, gentleness, and surrender within the individual and group psyches. They could charge and organize the heart's energy field in a grounded, humanized image of connection to and around a loving Christ. The internal egoic conversations became more sane and more balanced. The Word came to serve love. This challenged domination as the only option for social control. One role of Christ has been to materialize an internalized loving companion for the whole group.

Healing miracles in Jesus's story opened another grooming memory—the power of shared energy fields to strengthen the immune system and enhance emotional and physical well-being. This message has gotten lost in the idea of the miraculous. Somehow we grew really committed to the wrong

---

[31] John 1:1 (New Revised Standard Version).

question: "What do I believe?" A better question is "What is challenging my understanding?" People persistently doubt and dismiss the healing power of shared energy fields because it may not be a permanent fix. High levels of shared energy in a peak experience can move and remove disease in the body. That level of injected energy may last for three to five days. After that, if the body shifts back into an old, familiar energy state that originally supported the disease, the disease will likely return. This reversion has created a distrust of and disbelief in energy healing. The maintenance of higher energy fields that support persistent healing may not be compatible with exploitative relationship patterns.

Healing the Herder's Wound in the Masculine Psyche

The original wound from the loss of inherent belongingness we felt in grooming practice left the masculine psyche much more vulnerable to the denial of inherent worth from herding. The original wound had to be treated first. The Christ image divinized the unconditional, restorative love that birthed our awareness of self and others through grooming. In him, an embodied form recalled that initial loving energy and could refocus the internal conversation on loving connection. This possibility had to open before we could assuage the compulsive fear about worthiness for life. This was a first step.

That capacity to have a loving internal conversation of nurture and forgiveness has expanded over centuries. In his book *The Better Angels of Our Nature*,[32] Steven Pinker does a marvelous analysis, with insight and statistics, demonstrating that the level of violence in human community has diminished through history. He shows how human thought processes have expanded the practice of reciprocity into ever-larger arenas of relationship. The knife edge between violence and civility has become more conscious and the potential for making caring choices has grown. If we appropriately incorporated Pinker's history and insight on violence and morality into adolescent education, I could foresee a broadening of choices for the masculine psyche, with less to prove and more to cherish in the masculine identity.

---

[32] Pinker, Steven. *The Better Angels of Our Nature: Why Violence Has Declined*. New York: Penguin, 2011.

Christ's story demonstrated how we had embodied a belief equating death with not being chosen because of herding practices. Our subconscious conflict about killing animals we had nurtured (Abraham's pain) now had a new symbol: Christ on the cross. Shrouded in mystery, our potential for staying present to our pain, facing it, and healing opened into an expanded space when the symbol became external. God still held the projection for us, but it wasn't buried. It had risen. We could slowly hold the mystery as we reclaimed some ownership of worthiness. But for full healing, a Second Coming was anticipated.

As I expand my space for holding the pain and violence that underlie so much of the masculine identity, I have hopeful questions; but I feel like I see through a glass darkly. My most daunting question is this: What meanings can *equality* have within a subconscious framework that existentially identifies the opposite of dominance as death? Reason can expand our understanding and grow our potential for valuing equality and reciprocity in widening circles, but it cannot prevent the expression of repressed fear from rising to the surface. Can the behaviors that we name *white privilege and supremacy* that have arisen in our Judeo-Christian culture be a symptom, an enactment, of this harsh subconscious connection of death with masculinity? Healing the old wounds is the only safe way forward into a more complex community. How do we do that?

Can we as a people redo our relationship with herded and domesticated species? The *Humane Society* name puts the identification–projection circle right out there for contemplation. Can kindly respect for other species lead us out of some shadows within which we abuse ourselves and others? We need to recognize the limits and potential for error in identification and projection processes, as well as their power. Vegetarian humans might ask that herded species disappear in service to the human fear of death. Death is not an enemy. Nor is it the opposite of life. There is no life without it. Projecting our emotional relationship with death onto another species may create its own cruelty. We can find an example in the lingering deaths of beloved pets, when it is within our power to provide peace. If we made it a true priority to invest in minimizing the suffering of species that depend on us, would that investment pay off in greater happiness in human society? Would this communal choice open a path of escape from life dominated by fear of death? The choices are always nuanced boundaries. We cannot consciously encounter and embrace them unless the masculine and feminine within each of us can hold hands as we approach each limit. Dominance and nurture instincts shape human reality, creativity, and survival. For human health, personal wholeness, and full consciousness, we must rethink any experience where any individual is expected to "not be a woman" in order to fulfill a human role. A primary goal for a conscious life is to hold unity and separateness equally and minimize suffering in the name of either.

CHAPTER 8

Come Again?

Projection and identification are the mental processes that belong to us as a species. We also belong to them. Since the Renaissance, Western culture has adopted the scientific method to provide some defined structure in which we can subject a projection's value to an experiment to identify a consistent pattern or result. This is a more disciplined use of the same tools. We construct much of our reality with these tools. In this chapter we will look at three types of projections that have stretched our use of projection and identification into terrains for which they are ill equipped.

1. Projections into the mystery of time
2. Projections into nonbeingness, emptiness, and nothingness
3. Projections of unworthiness

Time and Eternity

Watching a toddler doggedly playing peek-a-boo, delightedly learning that things persist in time and space when unseen, we can get a feel for how our ancestors played with time. Choosing to engage with linear time meant choosing to engage with mystery. They sought to extend their exploration of the space-time grid that supports our sensed reality into realms of the infinite, which we can only approach with imagination.

We focus a lot of our fear and our hope on eternity, toward an unknown and unimaginable future. Many look to eternity for future salvation—for relief from life's trials. The possibility of interacting with linear time provided an entrance into a new and wondrous wilderness of imagination in the Stone Age. Many could project the fulfillment of desire or the recovery of what was lost or dead into an imagined future. Those projections have enormous energy. We still explore the meaning and the range of our power to shape the future and to explore the past. We learned that wealth accumulation supported not just longevity but dominance power into old age. This was mind-boggling for the masculine, which had depended on the physical prowess of youth. What were the limits? To think beyond the Earth's cycles, beyond their dominance of daily life, seemed a magical liberation with undefined parameters. Humans could dominate nature in some areas, and each success led to more inflated imaginings. Confronting and accepting the limits takes a lot of experimenting. Wisdom is hard-won in this depth of time's mystery.

When someone dies, he or she is no longer here. Unity consciousness would have led egos to imagine going to some other place that's "not here." Stretching our reality frame into the unknown works for us. We still play peek-a-boo with time, fantasizing about time travel, freezing our bodies for future use, thrilling ourselves with archaeological finds, and developing new ways to control distribution of our wealth after death. We can readily understand heaven, reincarnation, and a Second Coming as healthy projections. All the energy of life on earth is about rising again and blossoming from the dirt. This can provide a bit of grounding for our imaginative play with time, but that imaginative play has no strong anchors. We should not judge this mental exploration. It is a true expression of creativity.

For the universe as we know it to manifest in consciousness, time and space dimensions must support its structure, just as a painting needs a canvas. But the relativity of time and space to light suggests that eternity as pure creative potential may be independent of any dimensional structure. So we can lightly hold our imaginative encounters with eternity. Dominance, as the instinct that protects existing boundaries, can really flounder in linear time. Nurture has driven our biggest success in projecting ourselves into the future. That success preserves, refines, and expands culture. Empires fall; power structures need to fall. Challenged by the next generation, the boundaries of identity need to shift. In our exploration of linear time beyond our embodied experience, feminine nurture instincts that preserve the healthy learning and wisdom of cultures would best guide our projections.

Separation and Emptiness

Fear of death is a major theme that separates us from wholeness in the present. It is an extension of our fear that the supporting community will expel us. From a projection of separation, of estrangement from our role within a healthy wholeness, we try to imagine nothingness in death. No hints in nature for that one! We feel it as an unfathomable loss—a loss greater than any we have so far experienced. This probes the farthest limits of separation, estrangement, and strangeness.

The oppositional separation in our psyches that herding choices necessitated did serve males with a longer life span. It created a dramatic rather than incremental change in life expectancy for the wealthy shepherd. As such, it would have held out hope and fueled desire for even more longevity. Death became more of an enemy and a defeat. Added to that, the split between the masculine and feminine sides, which the butchering of lambs engendered, would have increased the sense of loss and separation projected onto human death. With us having "died" to part of ourselves, the resulting darkness held hollow violence. The expectation that the boy "not be a woman" in the butchering process separates him from trust in life, trust in regeneration, and trust in transformational wholeness. It can barricade the soul as an isolated self in need of justification.

Separation or isolation is hell for all primates. PBS's *Frontline* did a comprehensive set of documentaries on isolation that reference Harry Harlow's rhesus monkey experiment. "In one notorious study from the 1950s, University of Wisconsin psychologist Harry Harlow placed rhesus monkeys inside a custom-designed solitary chamber nicknamed 'the pit of despair.' Shaped like an inverted pyramid, the chamber had slippery sides that made climbing out all but impossible. After a day or two, Harlow wrote, 'most subjects typically assume a hunched position in a corner of the bottom of the apparatus. One might presume at this point that they find their situation to be hopeless.' Harlow also found that monkeys kept in isolation wound up 'profoundly disturbed, given to staring blankly and rocking in place for long periods, circling their cages repetitively, and mutilating themselves."[33]

Primatologist Frans De Waal speaks to how we as humans resemble primates in our intense need for social interaction: "Next to death, solitary confinement is our most extreme punishment."[34] Isolation creates paranoia and violence toward the self. We prefer pain to nothingness. Similarly, *Frontline* reports, "Solitary has been linked to a range of psychological problems, including depression, hallucinations, self-harm and suicide. In 2011, United Nations Special Rapporteur on torture, Juan E. Méndez, called for an absolute ban on solitary confinement lasting more than 15 days."[35]

How does fear of isolation color our fear of death? Death itself is part of life, a rich part of the dance with time. Our death does not and cannot separate us from life on earth. There is no "after" life. Life persists. How we imagine its transformations does not have a true or false value. The mental play of our imaginings can express trust in life or disconnection from it. We can come to the self-understanding that our fear of separation is part of the nature of the communal immune system we call *consciousness*. It does not need to translate into death, for in truth, we are not alone. In truth, all emptiness holds creative presence.

Unworthiness

A third dangerous projection for a future salvation or Second Coming belief dynamic is the theme of being chosen. Living into this projection can create a crushing burden of fear and self-doubt. Relying on being chosen causes problems because it is inherently insecure. It is not unconditional. Life itself is worthy, and entering into it unconditionally drives the power to live in love and freedom. Being chosen relies on judgment. The human understanding of genetic manipulation in breeding animals generated an

---

[33] Breslow, Jason. What Does Solitary Confinement Do to Your Mind? *Frontline*. April 22, 2014. https://www.pbs.org/wgbh/frontline/article/what-does-solitary-confinement-do-to-your-mind.

[34] De Waal, Frans. *Our Inner Ape: A Leading Primatologist Explains Why We Are Who We Are*. New York: Riverhead Books, 2005, p. 6.

[35] Nolan, Dan, and Chris Amico. Solitary by the Numbers. *Frontline*. April 18, 2017. https://www.pbs.org/wgbh/frontline/article/solitary-by-the-numbers.

arena of judgment about worthiness for life; that judgment inevitably reflected back into human society and self-definition within that society. With it came varying projections into an afterlife dependent on group allegiance or behavior. The question about worthiness for life or for an afterlife emerged from our judgment over another species—the worthiness of young male herded animals to live and reproduce.

A limited interpretation of dominance in evolutionary survival drives a modern, unhealthy "chosen" projection on our human life in community. Survival of the fittest requires the question "Fittest for what?" Adaptation is a response to a time and place. It is not a linear ascension. It is a creative process that calls forth a diversity of life in all niches of the planet. The value of different herded animal breeds comes in their adaptation to specific environments and markets. The purpose of mammals' dominance instinct is not simply "power over." It is about "adaptation to." It is about desire for the new creation or new relationship. Dominance and submission are choices that the sensate self supports. Desire is not single minded. "Fittest for what?" remains a moving target. Creative change is inherent to essence. Many people misheard and misused Darwin as heralding and advocating a harsh culling in the name of dominance.

Herders cultivated judgment in exercising control of breeding for set goals. But shepherds culled the majority of male lambs, not just those they judged inferior. They chose few male lambs for breeding. They killed the majority before they could mate. Castration could extend their lives a bit to accommodate slaughter times; they spread slaughter times out more conveniently to grow meatier carcasses, but most rams were not long worthy of resources. Since shepherds culled so many, herding judgments often determined worthiness a bit arbitrarily, and this level of judgment reflected back on humanity. It also projected onto and through the community relationship to unity consciousness, to God. The inherent instability of the "chosen" relationship required a covenant or agreement subject to interpretation. This added new meaning to the incomprehensibility of God's mystery. This projected life-and-death judgment assaulted unity consciousness. The shepherd's projections left little room for the masculine soul to find a secure resting place in a feeling of belonging. Judgment rained down. The tightly compartmentalized nurture instincts were not freely available for projection onto a Father God, nor onto any father–son relationships. Being chosen puts you in a tenuous position that can lead to ugly projections of the object for which you may be chosen—life or death, inheritance, slavery, or banishment.

Jesus has made it accessible for many of us to heal our wound of separation and shame, the wound that originated in the loss of grooming's shared energy fields. Many have found him the intimate, personal companion who brought health and sanity to their internal landscape and conversation. The "body of Christ" sourced a sense of tribal unity that could embrace the other lovingly and with forgiveness. People could honor feminine nurture within the community and once again modulate the dominance instinct within a loving persona. The incarnate presence of unconditional love held open a new space—a space in which to recall the essence of the original human connection, and the healing power of touch. Internal conversation as well as community structures opened up to try to reconcile the fear and separateness that the law and cravings for attuned connection embodied. It laid groundwork for potential healing, but it has been a slow conversation and conversion. Violence has slowly decreased over the centuries, and people have named and explored it. Punishment has been tested to its limits for effective impact, with variable results. There is language for *inhumanity*, and for the dissonance of crude human dominance behavior that disrupts and distorts human community. We have started to become conscious of the power that touch has for mental, emotional, and physical health. But we still approach healing slowly. It can't quite happen yet.

Still Waiting

A second wound keeps us separated within and without; a wall of compartmentalization that originating in herding. For as long as and to the extent that the masculine and feminine in our minds and bodies, our families, and our communities remain estranged and violently separated from each other, both sides are imprisoned. Neither side is free to come fully into the light of consciousness, and each must act in the shadows. Neither the masculine nor the feminine identity can reveal its power and beauty.

The Second Coming is the healing, waiting ensconced in a powerful symbol until we are ready. Christ has the great gift to display and carry that second wound for us until we can consciously manage it. The crucifixion's image holds our wholeness's internal death that herding choices occasioned.

We identify with the animals we slaughter and project the violence in that relationship back onto our species. It is held for us until we can be present to it with the maturity to manage interspecies relationships. We approach the time when we must face it for our survival. We have the discernment. We can manage our fear of ourselves. For fear lies in our capacity to harm ourselves and others within family, community, and the environment. It is a real fear. Being a member of the super-predator species puts one in danger of identifying and projecting as a predator.

We can also project and identify as a caregiver with attunement to wholeness. We can now take the full meaning of the Last Supper into our conscious awareness, and we can forgive ourselves. How can we affirm the sacred unity of consuming and being consumed with loving kindness? This is not a task for the immature, for the mind afraid of death, or for the self-absorbed. It does not come easy even in a community of love, but it is possible.

Reconnecting the feminine and masculine in peaceful sharing and in nonviolent, respectful conflict is key to our fulfillment as human creatures. Masculine dominance defines our success as primates, and that has been a powerful force. The feminine energy of nurturance defines our humanness, our culture, and the unique power of interconnection that can organize the masculine power with insight, and with creative direction that serves life on earth. Together, we can conceive and implement a wholeness that allows the joy of attunement to serve our souls, leading them out of the desert of fearful separation. We need to free the masculine from chronic fear about his inherent value. Protection of planetary life, of internal life, of personal value, and of healthy connection is a role for the masculine to now accept in unity with the feminine. We have no significant exterior threats. We have become our own most threatening enemy, manifesting our fear of death beyond our species' war instincts and onto all relationships with our whole environmental support system.

Our social structures treat young men as expendable. Dominance instincts under threat lead the masculine to try to minimize competition. Know the motive by the effect, not the justification. Military service may be glorified verbally on a national holiday, but veteran care is not a top priority in our national budget. There is no educational imperative to nurture all our young men into valued places in our society. Prisons are used to disempower young black men; and we as a nation display no intention of nurturing them into our society. We encourage a system of violence that will then be used as justification. Warehousing young men in camps in the Middle East for generations was a recipe for terrorism. Young men cannot grow to serve life as fathers in desolate conditions. We must infuse healthy competition with respect and the promise of being nurtured into productive roles that serve life. We cannot leave our male children to serve death in their isolation, through war, crime, suicide, jail, or addiction, or else we will all live in fear—fear for and of the masculine in all of us. Dominance can be focused as a predatory instinct, which equates failure with death, or it can be focused as a protective leadership force for maintaining deep community connection.

The word *inhuman*, or *inhumane*, is a telling use of language. War is obviously a very human behavior. We have a depth of insight to mine here from our language. In its use, we perceive *inhuman* to separate us from less-than-human behaviors, but its form bespeaks the lie. These things are in or part of our humanness. Our inhumanness leads us directly into conscious presence with our evolving nature, deeper into conscious awareness of the boundary and connection choices that we hold for ourselves. Our powers of identification and projection can carry us anywhere—into fear or into love.

Realizing that identification with the herders' culling process has transferred terrible fear and anxiety back into human masculine self-valuing is a first freeing step. The shakiness of social structure in evolution from grooming to language made us especially vulnerable to questions of our own value. We had no firm framework to face the emotional complications of extending our familial nurturance boundary to prey species. In the process we abandoned our attunement to life and instead trapped ourselves in fear-based control. How do we reclaim attunement?

We can recognize and make conscious our relationships with other species within a holistic mind—a mind that both thinks and senses into unity. Shared discernment from within attunement is critical. The many domesticated species that serve our needs depend on us. We can honor their essence and their role with gratitude by providing them with lives we honestly deem to have inherent value and with compassionate deaths. Our powers of projection and identification can then serve us well to honor our essence in attunement with life and living food, and a sacred honoring of death. There is no easy right relationship, but we can create a holy relationship, subject to a constant presence of compassionate discernment, using both sides of our brains in concert.

CHAPTER 9

Growing Our Attention

A truly wonderful blessing from the grooming experience was the opportunity to play with our attention. We humans easily capture, coerce, channel, and focus our attention, often with little awareness of choice. Conscious flexibility of attention is a freedom we would do well to cultivate. The holy sense of connection to the earth our hunting ancestors held in their attention field need not be a lost art. It can reappear in a new context with a fresh motivation. We can cultivate new multisensory attunement skills as part of creating a culture that serves quality of life and health. Snorkeling, diving, and hiking with caring and nurturing attunement to the environment can be a start. Yoga has much to teach us about embodied presence. Walking meditation, dance, and forest bathing can each open perceptual skills. Music can hone a sensitivity to vibration that can grow in subtlety and connect us with the fullness of creation. Energy attunement to light can grow a sensitivity to subtle radiation as well as all the nuances of reflection. Meditation and mindfulness practices have great value to discernment skills as well as health. It is critically important that they connect the mind and body with love. Sometimes, people use them with judgment against the body, demeaning it as unworthy, temporary, or base. This orientation prevents people from being present in the now. It can deny faith in life and ascribe unity to another place and time, with a muddled ascendance that betrays *isness*, the sacred I AM embodied in all creation.

The hunter connects with all the energies of nature along with his energy as part of a whole event. He knows with his entire body. Connections are vivid, energetic, and subtle. Words and images quickly give way to the immediacy of experience—this moment, this light, this wind, and this particular animal's reactions. On the hunt, our ancestors cultivated a wide-open attunement to all the sensations their systems could manage. The hunting party had a shared high. Today we have little opportunity for that wide-open attention, except in war. It is seldom cultivated and frequently dishonored.

Instead, we carefully practice focused attention. In fact, we "pay" attention, treating our attention as a commodity for profit. We discipline it and keep it within tight limits. We may control its linear progression from left to right across page after page. We listen carefully to instruction and decode the contextual meaning of billions of sounds. We decode millions of symbols every day in service to our social context and surrender our attention to its media. Our attention is the most important commodity and currency produced for and by the culture. Many idioms express examples of its power, such as "Ignorance of the law is no excuse" and "Advertising pays." The community compels our focused attention as the price for belonging, for success and survival within its organization. And social complexity bombards us with competing stimuli. Wide-open attention does not serve productivity in most roles in our current culture. Yet in its primal essence, we find not only a realization of self but also joy and fulfillment; we find our embodied selves. It calls us back to our interdependence with nature. It stretches our senses and attunes our perceptions. As we remember, it accesses power in our bodies for movement, grace, and health. A place for it exists in our future, but we will have to consciously choose to open the space for it. Open attention and attunement in heart and mind can serve our soul, our essence, and our ultimate survival by reconciling us to a healthy life on earth. It can generate a holistic vision and enjoyment of healed selves, a sweet grace in our masculine–feminine dance, and comfortable freedom within the yin and yang.

An ecstatic high can come with open attention. It connects our soul to the earth's soul and our consciousness to our sensate body with keen joy. There is little room for judgment or demands as we fully encounter *what is*. We need to let our awareness flow freely within our bodies and the environment in a celebration of *what is*, lose our judgmental evaluations, and swim freely in beingness. When this happens, every cell can remember and feel whole. Healing happens. It creates vast internal space for love.

Today many in our society who are born with an inclination toward open attention are medicated to help them succeed in school. They are frequently our natural leaders. Labeling them as having attention deficit disorder, or ADD, presupposes only one valid mode of attention. Open attention is not a deficit; it provides a plethora of wisdom, happiness, and leadership. Focused attention is also a magnificent skill that serves us well around cultural input that requires judgment, but it frequently lacks holistic vision. Why not choose a healthy repertoire by cultivating both? We can cultivate both along with discernment about which mode we are using. Why can't we teach our children to use both—to be aware of using each mode and how to switch between modes? Can we teach our children to feel safe and free stretching their perceptions to both focus tightly and open widely? Growing the skill to recognize and move between different modes could heal addiction. How could consciously applying different modes to solving a problem, healing oneself, growing a relationship, and being a healthy part of the earth increase our capacity to experience our life together? One gift that might manifest is a wise awareness of the kind of boundaries that serve our health and happiness. By adeptly shifting our modes of perception, we could expand our problem-solving skills to include both masculine dominance and feminine nurturance boundary wisdom. This is mindfulness grown in service to life, in love of what is.

I propose that we and our children can learn to cultivate various modes for our attention. We may have access to a truer, broader freedom than any we have thus far pursued if we increase that repertoire. I propose that it is possible to increase our capabilities for choosing and practicing varied modes of attention without us depending on drugs to either constrict or expand consciousness. Dangerous situations in which our primal selves take over from our normal consciousness can trigger us into open attention. When that happens our powers and perceptions sharpen and increase. If we have the capacities there within us, can we learn to access them apart from the threat of death?

The fact that we usually need a threat to throw us into a state of open awareness can tell us something about the relationships within our psyches, or the power dynamics in intercellular communication. Can we choose to let love have more influence over those internal communications than fear? Can love provide more raw, energetic power than fear to support wholeness and life for human nature?

The hunter searches for resources that need not be prey animals, but anything that enhances and feeds life on any level. They need not be consumables. The hunter always has an opportunistic eye. He trusts that which he seeks is already connected to him in some way. Seeing the connection takes strenuous work. It requires willingness to fearlessly traverse unexplored internal and external space. There are vast resources within and without. When love for freedom and joy calls on us to plumb life, we will only increase our wisdom about life within all our complex cellular makeup. A genuine intention for full nonjudgmental presence is always rewarded.

Some Exercises

When we have open attention, nature restores and refreshes us in forests, oceans, mountains, streams, and glens. We find a resonance and soul rest in the energies of wild places. Our senses try to open in these spaces. We recall the ancient formative relationship to them. At first, you will find the following exercises easier in the wild, but try them anywhere.

Let's try to open the field of vision as hunters would by distributing attention over the full area of the visual field. Some do this automatically when driving, but many scan a focused beam of attention as they think necessary. So now, let's try to make the field as large as possible in wholeness, not scanned and joined as parts of a puzzle. The eyes relax into receiving, and slowly, the whole field comes into soft, equal focus. Hold your arms straight out to the sides. Wiggle a finger or thumb on each hand. Move your hands slowly forward so that both wiggles are visible at the edge of the field as you softly focus straight ahead. Then use the wiggles to try to expand the field a little—on both sides at once. While walking or sitting in the wild, or anyplace in nature, frequently use your hands in this way to train yourself to keep an open field. As you relax into the open field of vision, the acuity across the field will begin to equalize. You will become surer of your peripheral perceptions—more trusting in them. The amount of information you perceive in the field will increase a little. I have found that practicing in this way shifts my energy toward more clearly seeing my own life, my place in the world, and a unified sense of direction.

Similarly with hearing, try to open up to sound as the whole range of vibration. Feel the body sinking, relaxing into pure vibration. Hear the breeze on your skin. Hear the faraway sounds that orient you in space and time. Hear the echoes of your own steps in the earth. Can you hear your breath meet the atmosphere as you exhale? When inhaling, can you hear the atmosphere vibrating into and around your body? As you listen to your breath, can you hear the earth hearing your breath? Can you hear all the tumult of the blood racing in your arteries, as rhythmic and wild as the ocean? Listen to the leaves of a tree until you hear the branches, and then listen more deeply until you hear the trunk and roots. Lean on the trunk and step on the roots and hear with your cells. Listen to snow fall, knowing that its vibration is already part of you. Feel photons vibrate in your retina. Feel the vibration of your thought as you stretch for that sensation. Hear your doubt. Hear your fear. You are vibration. Hear here!

With practice, it becomes easier to enter these open states if you associate them with a physical signal. You might tug your earlobes to signal your body and mind to open hearing, as wiggling thumbs on outstretched arms can signal open vision.

Touch is the sense of primal choice—for movement toward or away, of acceptance or rejection. This sense chooses our boundaries and our transformation. All the other senses extend and refine the power of touch. In human hands, this sense has concentrated in marvelous ways. We have lost awareness of the most primal impulses of touch in a direct way because it has extended its reach so far, first with the remote sensing of smell, sound, and vision, and then with technology and communication tools. Reacquainting ourselves with our hands' inherent power is life giving and life restoring. We can easily confuse our hands' identity with tools since tools are a wonderful extension of their power. Hands are much more than tools. They hold the memory of our human essence, of every evolutionary choice, of every value we have reached out for, of every repulsion, rejection, and refusal. Hands taught the heart to love and the mind to create. We pass humanity to the next generation with our hands' loving touch. Being touched can call back to us our humanity when we lose it. We can listen to our hands, hearing their vibrations. They can sense the energy of relationships, and they know how to shift and refine it. Notice what your hands reach for; notice when they want to go into pockets. Read their wisdom. Inviting my hands to dance and my fingers to express has not only brought me intuitive access but also relieved arthritis. My fingers were clear with me about the price of going unrecognized and being pressed into slavish service. When that service connects to the heart, it is painless.

It is hard to use words that pinpoint the benefits of open attention. We feel the benefits, often as joy and trust in life. But I have become aware that this practice opens new connections in my brain. The internal compartmentalization becomes permeable. The walls between different parts of my life become short hedges. I see openings and opportunities, especially grand opportunities for gratitude. The dominance–nurture, masculine–feminine, and conservative–liberal dichotomies tend to merge, and I find opportunities to see both with love and understanding.

Greeting Intuition

Intuition is cellular knowing that has appeared in consciousness. Gut cells, liver cells, skin cells, or any cells may hold intuition. Consciously interpreting this information can be very tricky when it appears in an organ designed for social interaction. This interpretation often feels out of place. Wisely allowing and cultivating the pathways for this information is wildly tricky. The sensate body just contains too much information for the conscious mind to handle all at once. The body has real discrimination about how much and what information it can safely impart to consciousness. And consciousness has real discrimination about what it wants to know. With gratitude, we have to trust that the filtering works as best it can for our overall health and well-being in the moment. To expand conscious participation in the filtering decisions, our consciousness has to know how to respect moving boundaries, how to avoid generating fear about the future (the body will perceive the danger as occurring now), and how to listen with a nonjudgmental constancy of presence. To do these things requires great trust or faith in life, a willingness to stay present to the whole message with love and with simultaneous confidence in the knowing and in the not knowing completely. This may be the deeper meaning in the law of love.

Fear has its place, and we must thank it for its genuine protection. Within the culture supported by word and law, people exploit fear for power over others. It lives within us and has a home in our hearts when it should live at the boundary, on guard to protect our happiness. For our fear to corrode our happiness from within is a terrible aberration. Grooming brought us together in community in a way that cultivated feelings of safety. Language does not inherently hold the power to do that; in fact, it too easily relies on fear to maintain communal connection. There is no peace, only lessening of antagonism. Forgiveness and acceptance are hormonal processes, not thought processes. They must be cultivated as such. Presence to ourselves in love is the necessary practice for presence to the other.

Love for ourselves, for all our internal dynamics, including dying, is a path to wisdom. Entering our individual death as a healthy process for the species and the planet and for our essence is a necessary part of the balance. Time is a mystery that we live within together. It is not an individual challenge. Viewing death as an enemy imbues death with unnatural, demonic power over the quality of our life and turns self-love into disconnection and away from unity consciousness.

CHAPTER 10

Extending the Internal Conversation

While driving to work alone one summer morning before dawn with a long cornfield on my right, I became aware of a conversation going on in my head. One voice said, "There was a foot back there." Another voice said, "Don't be silly. There was no foot." As far as I knew, I hadn't seen a foot. I had no visual image of a foot, yet I turned my car around and used my headlights to scan the edge of the cornfield. And there I saw a foot sticking out. I investigated it and found that the foot belonged to a man who was either asleep or unconscious along the edge of the road. When I roused him, he jumped up in a panic and ran away screaming, probably under some chemical influence.

Back in my car and continuing on my way to work, I revisited the mental conversation that had led me to investigate something I had not consciously seen. I realized that my subconscious—the voice that said, "Don't be silly"— had tried to protect me from actually stopping on a dark road to investigate; my subconscious feared for my safety. When I realized this, it made me a bit upset. I didn't want fear to filter and censor the visual input of my awareness. This led me to an understanding: I had to willingly assume a greater conscious responsibility for my safety (one that my subconscious could abide) if I hoped to gain my primal self's trust.

I came to accept that the part that had seen the foot but kept it from my consciousness had real wisdom, and I was grateful. I understood that my ability to be fully present in my life depended on how well I could apply the law of love with myself as well as with others. At the time, I had no idea how to go about engaging my whole self, but beginning the process turned out much easier than I at first anticipated. Just holding the intention led me into a presence to myself that is both very flawed and imperfect and wondrously fulfilling and somehow adequate. I got better at self-protection, though I failed often. In the failure, I found that the intention to listen and be present was enough for love, forgiveness, communication, and trust to happen within me—not trust in the sense of a rigid dependency free of any possibility of betrayal; just trust in the possibility of all the voices being heard and honored. My sensate self has much more skill than my ego does for accepting the messiness of life.

Love and Dominance in a Triune Brain

The sections of our brains (the brain stem, the cerebellum, the cerebrum and neocortex) that grew around each other through evolutionary time are still in dynamic cocreative development. They all have their own wisdom. And seniority is to be respected. The longest history of survival adaptations through eons of change deserves honor. The primal or reptilian brain is the champion in speed and instantaneous communication between cells. It knows unity. In every nanosecond of now, it strives to serve life with fierce adaptability. The limbic midbrain led our species into feelings and emotions and grew group relationships. The forebrain with the neocortex, the youngster of the three, played with the powers of consciousness and rationality by which we define ourselves.

The dominance instinct was a prominent force in shaping and governing the mammalian brain for all stages and structures. As each part developed over time, its benefits merited the dominance position in the arenas of its development: survival, emotions, and thought (a gross oversimplification, but handy and to the point). Dominance determines communication between the parts of the brain, carefully controlling and filtering information to limit or enforce power. Dominance necessitated a natural, internal, conflictive dimension to brain communication among the three parts in order to best serve life. Deceit and secrecy can be the most natural and healthy way to respond to demands that threaten safety. Shutting down a communication pathway may be preferable to internal war or overwhelm. The primal brain can knock one unconscious if it senses an intention that will threaten the system. Breathing and heart rate can come under only limited conscious control in ways that can serve the organism's well-being. A child blocks conflicting information about parents when that is necessary to allow for growth. The roles of different brain parts and functions frequently conflict; group survival, species survival, and individual survival often struggle in conflict and in a dance of secrecy. If group and individual interests conflict dangerously, it is often wiser to keep the conflict out of sight, buried in the subconscious parts. Sleep provides some necessary balance restoration.

An interesting and usually wrongly interpreted example is the fainting reaction that can happen after blood donation. The primal body, sensing a drop in blood volume, quickly drops its blood pressure. This very good survival response is designed to prevent the body from bleeding out. It often results in fainting or dizziness. Even without sensing imminent external danger, the primal brain is wise to try to take control from the will in this way. It demonstrates an evolutionary advantage. Men, especially, can interpret this event as a weakness rather than as the sign of a strong and responsible body. In this situation, it is possible to construct a loving, grateful, reassuring internal communication that can prevent the fainting response. When communicating with the primal parts of yourself, remember that you must use very literal language. Verbal understanding usually meets a four-year-old's level. You can best send messages and intentions on the breath. Some deep, calming breaths at the beginning of the blood donation send reassurance to the body that the blood loss will be limited and safe. This internal conversation can include deep gratitude for the rich blood that has been produced and the intention to share a little of that bountiful richness. When finishing, breathe a grateful message that the gift is complete and all is well. Then breathe with grateful confidence that the cells easily know how to find a new equilibrium, truly enjoying a moment of patience while they do just that. The conversation has a loving tone. Fear will send the primal parts back into survival mode, quickly subvert internal trust, and drop blood pressure. A conquering hero's dismissive attitude that judges this as a weakness will be rightly dismissed in favor of a survival instinct. Taking the tone of a wisely protective and deeply respectful father can work best.

This simple example sends the message that we can and must apply the law of love or compassion, which infuses most religious traditions, in our brains if it is to happen without. If we cultivate a humble self-love that acknowledges the body's true place in unity, we can reduce the trickery, opportunism, and wasted energy of imagined fear through a real internal communication that can then project outward.

A more tragic case is the true cruelty in not listening to the internal struggles that cause cancer cells to try to adapt to stressful demands that do not serve life. The cells give up after an exhausted repertoire of intelligent adaptations and resort to wildly reproducing without direction. On their own, they manifest the fearful, deadly confusion of multiple rude physical, emotional, and spiritual stresses. And they try to do this in secret, in the terror of separateness, giving up on unity. They forget who they are within wholeness and become cancerous, and with that naming, at their discovery, the whole organism at last hears their terror. Listening deeply to the body beneath the fear and sensing the lost connections can create spontaneous remission. The common healing practice of the twentieth century has been to bring the whole body close enough to death that all the parts surrender and reconcile, coming together in mutual support to choose life, if that is energetically possible.

Beyond Dominance

Attunement to our internal bodily state is not the original cultivated purpose of our egoic consciousness. It does not even seriously try to meet the body on holy ground, as evidenced by the mechanistic and chemical structure the ego ascribes to the body without acknowledging inherent intelligence in its complexity. The sensate body would have been derelict to concede power to these sluggish, ephemeral neural networks before they developed some "sense." Their purpose was to serve the group. As witnessed during rich moments of attunement (when the ego only gets in the way, such as when an athlete is "in the groove"), the sensate body knows itself in time and space. The original purpose of neocortical neural circuits was to connect and serve a shared consciousness within the primate group, within the tribe—a tribal immune system. But the law of love has laid enough groundwork over thousands of years for a freeing conversation between body and mind to be carried on deep within. Both agendas, group solidarity and connection to the individual body, need to be honored equally. Our primal selves can be appreciated with awe, rather than treated as base or unworthy. They can be heard for their deep wisdom and drawn as a gentle witness into a healthy lifestyle. And from that *heartfelt* conversation, deliciously fruitful attunements to all species and to the wholiness of life on this planet can sprout and flourish.

The shift in energy this requires is not great in volume but subtle in its movements. It is interwoven with ancient remembrance of attunement to our interconnections with all that is, for we are the same fabric. As humans, we have been called to stretch beyond dominance interaction into a unified strength for fullness of life. We can do this and live and die in radiant connection—in unity. Loving connection to the sensate body is the humble holiness of unity. Compassion is birthed in the senses and, there, wisdom can show herself in true connection—a mutuality of honoring. At first, in small arenas of trust and listening, the sensate body will begin to share its riches. A hopeful name for this process has been Christ. Another is the Buddha. Love will manifest in the group with the energy of its individual internalization.

CHAPTER 11

Attunement

Attunement has such a vast, measureless fullness of meaning that words can only provide hints about it. Within the domain of words, poetry has the most currency with attunement. Please have patience with my words. Take them as hints of a state of beingness, not limitations.

Consider the following experiences.

- Gliding in whiteness and exhilaration down a ski slope
- Shooting baskets on the days the body "just does it" without missing and the doing shuts down analysis
- Being in wordless presence with another, not knowing what is carried on the full flow of energy moving in the space between but receiving it with awe
- Feeling such deep gratitude that the only expression of it is flowing tears
- Watching a lambing on a freezing night and knowing warmth and cold essentially

These experiences flow into oneness, each a taste of unity consciousness. They all are sensate bodily experiences, enjoyed by the mind as observer in simple presence. Within their quality of oneness, we feel truly whole. All internal conflict is blessedly quiet. There is only now. These moments just happen. We can create some conditions to make them more likely, but the more we try to create or recreate them, the more elusive they can become. These moments have a mysterious opportunism to them.

The sense of unity will usually have a predominant focus. It may focus on oneness with one's own body, oneness with nature, oneness with another, or oneness with God or with any other energy of mutuality. Our conscious mind opens to share an experience with the sensate body. The raw energy of life leaves our egoic mind in awe. Consider that the egoic mind is struck dumb when it tunes into only one channel of unity energy. The sensate body manages all the energy channels simultaneously. Oh, the boundary dynamics to explore!

Let's focus on attunement to touch. Hands have a special power. The image of the hand of God as a human hand expresses truth about the power for love and creativity within our hands. In ordinary consciousness we often experience hands as mere mechanical tools. In truth, they connect our heart to our mind, and most often they offer the best connection between those two organs. By grooming each other, our hairy ancestors' hands learned to connect with the other in love as acceptance, affection, forgiveness, comfort, and healing. Grooming's touch generated a highly tolerant and patient energetic field within the group, even while dominance was given its due in maintaining leadership and protective organization. Patience is usually counterproductive for maintaining leadership. Decisiveness and quick response are an imperative of leadership in the wild. But the domain of grooming engendered a safe, patient, contemplative space for creativity, sharing, and teaching. The sense of touch, already highly adept at creating boundaries with immediacy, now had the space and time within grooming to play with those boundaries in new awareness. Opposable thumbs may have first served a communal immune system against parasites and then projected the skills of focused consideration and deftness into tool making. Learning the characteristics of different kinds of wood and stone allowed humans to handle things less impulsively and more contemplatively, to see things in multiple contexts, and to see within an object seeking out its essence. This kind of patient mind is not instinctive within a pure dominance survival structure. Nurture and love are essential to patience, but perhaps not sufficient. A contemplative time or practice may be a vital component.

A sense of touch at the cell boundaries defined the earliest cocreative cellular relationships. Long before the specialization of nerves, touch led cellular biological evolution on a magnificent trip of relational creativity, defining layer upon layer of interdependence. From distinct internal organs to interspecies relationships, touch brings boundary formation, boundary recognition, boundary respect, and boundary defense into being and into shared consciousness.

The word *manipulation*, a derivative of the Greek word for "hand," has shadowed meanings. Boundaries can be dishonored and connections used in hurtful ways, but cellular touch has less potential for deceit than words. Boundary definition seems to need to rest in the realm of touch. Our knowing by touch can extend throughout all the cells in our bodies in a direct way. Touch holds the oldest wisdom about communication and boundaries. Touch issues from a well of intelligent, energetic connection that could serve our consciousness in ways that we now need. Can our consciousness issue the invitation that will connect to these powers with enough love and respect that our personal and species' organisms will be willing to soften some boundaries and include our conscious minds in evolutionary wisdom?

Many hands dance to accompany speech. The more emotional investment one has in speech, the more animated one's hands become. Self-expression by writing with a pen or keyboard can concentrate a lot of energy in the hands. The same repetitive movements as labor without a heart connection or with resentment could quickly trigger pain such as carpal tunnel syndrome or arthritis as energy drains from the hands with no refill from the heart. How do we refill and honor our hands as sacred parts of the self, not tools? Hands have their own wisdom, so it is well worth listening to our hands. Letting them dance is one way that I do this. It has provided an effective start to a conscious relationship with my hands. It gave them permission to speak, and it trained me to watch and listen with appreciation free from an agenda. Being present to my hands has become part of my being in the moment. I notice where they instinctively reach—to a tree trunk, to a dog I want to pat, to a sore spot that I hadn't noticed, to my chest when I need to ground myself in a difficult situation, or to a hand, a shoulder, or a cheek of someone I love. My hands love it when I breathe with my diaphragm. They feel a bit cut off when I breathe from my chest.

The energy in my hands will tell me when someone close by is in distress, even if I see no outer signs at first. I feel my hands become heavy with increased blood flow, and my fingertips begin to tingle. This is a primal response to reach out and restore the tribe to peace. When I follow that instinct—that is, when I can follow it with a respect for boundaries—some resolution or healing will usually happen. This is not a miracle; it is human nature—a very real human potential that lives beneath consciousness. This happens all the time without our awareness. We heal each other without conscious intent, without an agenda, but just with presence. Presence is creative energy flowing. Our hands are immanently in the now, connected to isness. We add our own conscious intent and focus it in loving effectiveness, but always from a position of deferral to creative wisdom, the unity of all that is.

What is the invitation here? What is the risk? What effect do I wish for these words to have? Engaging our human energy potential with conscious control comes with fearsome boundary issues. It opens a whole arena for manipulation. There are good reasons to not go there. The energy boundaries we create are not visible, so we cannot easily detect trespassing. Energies come into resonance or dissonance to varying degrees from many inputs, and results can be surprising. If someone is suffering from cancer and his or her cells cannot remember their true essence, then an energy increase sourced through another person, even if well intentioned, could feed the cancer's growth. If the energy supplied through another imparts a frequency and intelligence that can help restore cellular memory and identity, then the cancer may heal. An energy that strengthens the cellular memory of true essence is healing. An energy of "life on any terms or at any cost" may not be healing in many situations even though it is an intense energy.

We can grow in wise and kind insight about shared energy fields that will have tremendous value to our lives, but total predictability is not a possibility. We will never choose consistently true or consistently wise boundaries. Many boundaries are subtle choices that have inputs from many dimensions. No matter how enlightened, our egos and conscious minds can never validly feel that they are on solid ground, totally right, or in control. We always operate in mystery in any domain, no matter what great lengths we may traverse to believe otherwise. It may be healthy that we have been discouraged or have discouraged ourselves from playing in this realm of subtle energy without humble self-knowledge. But perhaps the time has come to open our loving adult hearts to another try at a wiser, happier humanity. This is not magic or paranormal. It is the essence of life itself, passionately inclined to celebrate beingness itself, to create, transform, recreate, remember, adapt, and fall back into the void of pregnant chaos. It demands a huge shared trust in isness with all its faces. Our hands can hold ourselves and each other in awe as we would hold an infant—with deep, calm belly breaths so as not to be overwhelmed by the power of pure potential.

All is well. Choose freely.

CHAPTER 12

Being of Two Minds

Two instincts, dominance and nurture, drive the evolution of life on earth. Mammalian life in general and human life in particular are defined by the dance between these two instincts, the yin and yang of our reality perceptions. As they both cooperate with and oppose each other in a mystery of being, the most basic role of dominance is to preserve a genetic line, a memory of a pattern of being that deserves protection because it *is*. Isness is its bottom line and defines its authority.

As part of my perceptual limitation, I find dominance often equates with ego, cruelty, and oppression, while nurture implies care, kindness, and culture. I struggle to remember dominance as protection and preservation—that the dominance instinct anchors and defines identity for both the individual and the group. Personally, I have found it very difficult to stay openly present to the dominance instinct without feeling it as a powerful force in opposition to love. It takes a big effort to demand of myself an open mind and heart with which to experience dominance energy without that judgment. I need help with that. I fail and I try again and I invite the reader to expand my efforts.

While these two primal instincts shape most of our human behavior and experience, our conscious minds seldom directly acknowledge the presence, the power, or the subtleties of their roles. While their conflict plays out in male–female relationships, conservative versus liberal political ideologies, compartmentalized versus holistic problem solving, child-rearing customs and precepts, justice and rehabilitative social systems, religious beliefs and structures—in all compelling aspects of our lives—our consciousness cannot or does not address them directly, for dominance also seems to control our access to self-knowledge. Our souls are complicit in keeping the relationship between these two instincts below the level of conscious thought. Will we reach a level of wise maturity where we can be directly present to these instincts and lessen our torment? What will that take? As I have already discussed, acknowledging the split in our brains, as the herding experience cemented, provides one source of healing. As I try to stay present in love, other connections do surface that I would like to share.

We name and try to counter abuses; bullying might be an example, as distinct social or individual problems. We do not directly observe, discuss, or own the primal power of these instincts—the actual dynamism of their action within us individually and as a group. These instincts may show real wisdom in not giving up any direct power to rational consciousness as long as they are held in shaming judgment. These instincts not only predate consciousness, but evolved consciousness to serve their ends. That is exactly analogous to our present fear of creating an artificial intelligence that will one day enslave us. Our shadowed acknowledgment of the role of dominance gets projected onto machines. So how can human consciousness serve life better by getting to know and acknowledging these instincts? In the future, as genetic manipulation by human judgment becomes commonplace, how will the dominance instinct manifest and support nurturance? Maybe we should more proactively engage our internal dynamics with loving attention before we act them out in that arena.

Dominance is a magnificently powerful and brutal force. It is a big, successful instinct. On one hand, we chafe and quake under the unfairness of its rule; on the other, we revel in conquest and in a perceived grand ascent of human mastery. Naming it an instinct does not dishonor its sacred power or holy purpose. Its competitive dynamic works on all levels, especially between its own opposing interests. Individual survival and group survival always compete against each other in betrayal versus loyalty, greed versus mutuality, scapegoating versus cooperation, and shame versus arrogance. Dominance's purpose is to protect the isness that survives. It does not freely surrender itself to discernment.

Destruction, including self-destruction, is inherent in the dynamic. Dominance can easily eat its own tail, creating cycles of self-destruction as it serves its own energy. In suicide and suicide bombing, it can strive to dominate by guilt or terror without seeing the death-over-submission choice in these scenarios as insanity. When dominance no longer serves isness, but serves its own dynamic, that is insanity.

Let's look at sportsmanship to gain some beginning insight that will light a path forward into a conscious encounter with dominance. Sports healthily express the physicality and competitiveness of our nature. They are an important source of sanity and balance for many young humans, so distanced from their original physical design. In a sense, sports function as a great cultural expression of the nurture instinct because they grant a gracious space to experience, enjoy, and manage the dominance instinct in a healthy way. The enforced limits to its expression are unique to each sport. Learning to manage the dominance desire to win at all costs and violate what we define as healthy limits is a normal part of the experience. This is the reason for referees and umpires. Sports rules may be the best examples of the double message around dominance that pervades our living culture. Often, a number of violations are carefully calculated to balance the benefit of the dominance drive without triggering an unacceptable punishment. Penalties control the violence of a game in a way that cultivates a skilled awareness of trade-offs.

Our male ancestral primates had confrontations for dominance that usually ended with one party signaling submission and retreating; but sometimes they fought to the death. The old dominance drives are still with us. Learning to be a good loser in sports helps directly address their management. With a subtle shift in language, children and adults could learn to discern these instincts that are always operating within all of us. They are not bad. They are *instincts*. We can observe them, not just stuff them out of sight. As we learn about how they operate within us, we will begin to understand the complex boundaries that we have created around the individual within various groups. We will need to limit behaviors with rules as a crude bottom line, but keeping the center of our focus on unity of intention, unity of purpose, and a powerful communal projection of oneness grounded in forgiveness.

Rules and their enforcement express dominance in service to nurturance without really giving up any power. The illusion is that controlling behavior controls the instinct. Rules work to the degree that the instinctive drive allows without relinquishing its cover. By learning to address dominance not with a good-or-bad judgment but as exploration of the self, one can aim for transformation. Just verbally recognizing the primary purpose of sports organizations is to express the nurturing instinct and grow healthy competitive skills will prevent equating being a man with not being a woman. Thus far in the grand design of creative, evolutionary flow, a system of crime and punishment may have been sensibly preferable to the kind of conscious exposure that would constrain dominance's inherent opportunism. Do we have the courage to explore dominance and nurture beyond this level and to consciously invite both to the table in any important discussion?

Double messages pass between fathers and sons—fathers tell sons to be powerfully masculine and to be good boys. A "boys will be boys" wink of pride can simultaneously accompany punishment and shame for expressing aggression in the wrong place at the wrong time. These signals leave little or no room for self-confident wisdom. People accept this dissonance, reinforced in herding's demand for emotional distance, as part of the culture of masculinity, at least in Western civilization. Integrating within masculine roles poses a terrible challenge.

Both sexes operate from the masculine and from the feminine; we all have a hard time engaging both at once. The double message to the masculine fiercely reinforces the inner separation between masculine and feminine in the conscious functioning of both sexes.

As I tried to come into loving presence in my exploration of dominance, a marvelous book by Iain McGilchrist[36] helped me observe my own left-brain compartmentalization around this instinct. He provides an enlightened and comprehensive analysis of the physical and cultural aspects of the left–right brain enigma. All my categorizations between the left- and right-brain hemispheres—masculine versus feminine, dominance versus nurture, compartmentalization versus holism—are valid as metaphors, but not definitive. He confirms that the "versus" with which I struggled are a neurologic reality between the hemispheres manifested in their connectivity and inhibitory circuitry. His book is seminal and prophetic for our culture. For me, it validated my questions and gave me an invaluable gift. Through the flow of McGilchrist's book, I was led back to my early perception (described in my introduction) of seeing a spruce stump as vibrating light and energy.

---

[36] McGilchrist, Iain. *The Master and His Emissary: The Divided Brain and the Making of the Western World*. New Haven, CT: Yale University Press, 2009.

I began to see that perhaps the essential-boundary conundrum of that experience could inject some insight into the nature of the dominance and nurture instincts.

Seeing with Reflected Light

When I contemplated the boundary questions that seeing the tree stump as shimmering energy awakened in me, I considered whether our evolutionary choices created a vision modality that sees with reflected light rather than internal light. For example, infrared night-vision goggles allow us to see internal light. Boundary definition is not clear since the light extends out from the body. Edges are not clear in this light. Having the ability to see other animals at night would give one an advantage for surviving. This reminded me of a Sumerian image of a bull created over three thousand years ago, in which a golden aura outlines the body. Auras and halos were a common part of artistic depiction from earliest history through the Middle Ages. Some today see auras and energy fields. I have often perceived people as full of light or darkness, but without an actual image in my mind that allows me to see them in a concretizing way.

All of this leads me to question whether our species' development included an evolutionary choice to use reflected light to better discern and define boundaries. Perhaps some people have a vestigial capacity for perceiving internal light. The first known religious structure was *animism*, experiencing the divine in everything. Perhaps perceiving an inner light in all matter was part of that original experience of reality, an underlying unity consciousness. But creating and defining boundaries worked better with reflected light, and this may have been an evolutionary choice of much benefit. What if creating and discerning boundaries is the seminal role of the dynamic that we identify as the dominance instinct? Perhaps it functions as a perceptual tool that allows and creates separateness within unity by creating and enforcing boundaries. If so, it would have to be a tool of control that, by its nature, defines reality out of energy; its very purpose to reduce unity to manageable packets could provoke the otherness essential to consciousness, even to unity consciousness. In this context, I see a potential for holding dominance with great love. I can appreciate the amount of control needed to try to hold it all together amid constantly shifting creative energy. So a new question arises about the dominance instinct within and around me: "Can we make this relationship more fun?"

Creation as Boundary Generation

The first cell defined itself by creating a boundary. In the sea of transformative interaction between the energy systems of earth, air, fire, and water, a boundary defined a small unit of separateness and controlled the transfer of energy in and out of its small space. Cells agglomerated and formed new boundaries that defined new organisms with internal boundaries for specialized organs. Organisms organized into communities with individual and group boundaries, including sexual, social, and territorial. On some level, all boundaries were and are a choice—an evolutionary choice, a species choice, a habitat choice, a cultural choice, an individual choice. The whole creative process can be seen in terms of boundary creation, definition, and protection.

Humans defined new boundaries for wood and stone, creating edges that relied on intimate knowing of these materials' qualities. They created new boundaries in species relationships—new social and political boundaries, from tribal to national. They also created new boundaries around sound vibration, visual imagery, and movement, playing with beauty, pleasure, and meaning within boundaries. Some of these boundary definitions served immediate survival needs, and many served exploratory pleasure. Conscious boundary definitions had a place and a need for loving, intimate contemplation of the qualities of the energy involved in shaping a new boundary. Every consciously created boundary demands an investment of energy, time, and belief. All boundaries and all edges have some kind of permeability, malleability, and vulnerability. Humans must intimately know and experience clay and stone before they can make pots and weapons. All boundaries are energy transformed and transforming with a form that *is* in the now of creation. That isness is inherently worthy of being defined and defended.

When I contemplate all the boundaries, the edges, and the surfaces that surround me every day and acknowledge the human energy, thought, cooperation, and love that generated them, awe overwhelms me. I see walls, floors, ceilings, roofs, furniture, roads, fences, gardens, cities, nations, pipes, ponds, septic systems, dams, and lakes. The care, aesthetics, and love demonstrated in transforming materials with new surfaces and edges is awesome. The incalculable energy that the human race invests in creating boundaries is our defining characteristic. In fact, it might have earned us the *race* title, for we keep accelerating our creativity. We find dominance challenged and fierce in the creation of wealth, in marketing and distribution, and in labor and profit, but each successful enterprise begins with a contemplation, a nurtured idea, or a vision of connection. We must frequently "sell" this vision by justification in the dominance arena of profit. Our socioeconomic system can move ruthlessly, blindly, and magnificently within a dominance–nurture structure. We look for explanations, ideas, and ideologies by which we can avoid direct interaction with these forces. These are the instincts that drive our economy and our politics. They feel polarizing. Does economic theory predict behavior? Can we ask the right questions without directly naming dominance? Perhaps to directly ask how dominance and nurture drive the process would generate more insight and stability.

Within the paradigm of dominance as the force for boundary definition, it is possible to relinquish the dichotomy between dominance and nurture. It is possible to see the role of contemplative presence, of love, and of deep attention as the principal part of creative boundary formation in our human experience. By reflecting love (as attentive presence and valuing) back onto the dominance process of definition and defense of that isness, could we bring the dominance realm into the light of consciousness with enough appreciation and respect that it would not need to hide?

We can discern dominance responses in our canine companions and we use that understanding to train them. We are less discerning of how we respond to this instinct's prodding in our bodies, families, communities, and nations. Do we know why we choose submission in some circumstances and defiance in others? Do we trust power in others by the strength of its thrall or by its wisdom? When and why do we accept identification with a strong abuser as a healthy response? In our daily lives, can we see the subtler forms of dominance response, the energy in our solar plexus that makes us aware of the dominant males at a cocktail party, or our own eye movements and posture that show submissiveness? We can operate with great facility and skill in the dominance power arena and at the same time have no conscious awareness of the choices we are making. We need to consciously study dominance instincts and acknowledge them in a way that gives them their due, appreciates their survival wisdom, honors their leadership, and recognizes their dynamic workings in the psyche and in society. Only when we honor dominance will it come out of the shadows and lean its wisdom into cooperation. We must hear it well before it can feel safe in modulating power in the open. It must reunite with the awe and reverence with which the sensate self relates to being. If the projection of smallness and disconnectedness that dominance has so effectively practiced to create a controlled reality cannot be relieved of personal identification and held lightly, it will lead to self-defeat— to the loss of essential creative energy in the culture and in the species.

We can acknowledge and heal the ancient wounding adaptations that separated and compartmentalized the two sides of our brains around these two instincts, dominance and nurture. We can restore our inter-being with other species in open cooperation between the masculine and feminine sides of us in a way that projects a unified identity back onto our self-image. We can let ourselves off the hook. We can consciously engage both instincts in opening our internal communication, our conscious connection to our sensate self in exuberant enjoyment of life. Our species can relearn how to use touch to heal and explore the depths of our nature. It is too simplistic to allow the left side of our brain to reduce us to a mechanistic projection in our minds. We can thoroughly enjoy all the insight about the persistence of form and the persistence of creative change that our DNA exhibit. These insights represent a fresh blossoming of unity consciousness's creativity that somehow will find a way to enjoy all the uniqueness of itself. The longing for connection and the law of love inherent in human nature provide the most exciting path forward. We just have to remind the left brain that its true purpose is to create definition and separateness within unity. It is the tribute of a double-edged sword that dominance has functioned so well in its skills of definition and differentiation within our consciousness that we can think of ourselves as seeking unity without recognizing it as the ground of our being. The capacity to treasure all the forms in which creative energy manifests grants us the deepest felt connection to unity.

I pray this exploration leads to some new questions about ourselves. The right questions have more power than the right answers, so explore these ideas with hope and freedom. Expand them in love.

BIBLIOGRAPHY

Brennan, Barbara Ann. Hands of Light. New York: Bantam, 1988.

Breslow, Jason. What Does Solitary Confinement Do to Your Mind? *Frontline*. April 22, 2014. https://www.pbs.org/wgbh/frontline/article/what-does-solitary-confinement-do-to-your-mind.

Buber, Martin. *I and Thou*. Translated by Walter Kaufmann. New York: Scribner, 1970. Touchstone, 1996.

Burnham, Sophy. *The Ecstatic Journey: The Transforming Power of Mystical Experience*. New York: Ballantine Books, 1997.

Chomsky, Noam. *Language and Mind*. Cambridge, UK: Cambridge University Press, 2006.

Clutton-Brock, Juliet. *A Natural History of Domesticated Animals*. Austin: University of Texas Press, 1987.

Dale, Cyndi. *Energetic Boundaries: How to Stay Protected and Connected in Work, Love, and Life*. Boulder, CO: Sounds True, 2011.

Deacon, Terrence W. *The Symbolic Species: The Co-evolution of Language and the Brain*. London: W. W. Norton, 1997.

De Waal, Frans. *Our Inner Ape: A Leading Primatologist Explains Why We Are Who We Are*. New York: Riverhead Books, 2005.

De Waal, Frans. *Peacemaking among Primates*. Cambridge, MA: Harvard University Press, 1989.

Donald, Merlin. *A Mind So Rare: The Evolution of Human Consciousness*. New York: W. W. Norton, 2001.

Dunn, Robb. *The Wild Life of Our Bodies: Predators, Parasites, and Partners That Shape Who We Are Today*. New York: HarperCollins, 2011.

Eisler, Riane. *The Chalice and the Blade*. New York: Harper, 1987.

Feynman, Richard. *The Meaning of It All*. New York: Perseus, 1998.

Gerber, Richard. *Vibrational Medicine*. 3rd ed. Rochester, VT: Bear & Co., 2001.

Goldberg, Carl. *Speaking with the Devil: A Dialogue with Evil*. New York: Viking, 1996.

Humphrey, Nicholas. *The Inner Eye: Social Intelligence in Evolution*. New York: Oxford University Press, 2002.

Jablonski, Nina G. *Skin: A Natural History*. Berkeley, CA: University of California Press, 2006.

Jung, Carl G. *The Collected Works of C. G. Jung, Volume 9, Part 1: Archetypes and the Collective Unconscious*. Translated by Gerhard Adler and R. F. C. Hull. Princeton, NJ: Princeton University Press, 1969.

Kabat-Zinn, Jon. *Coming to Our Senses*. New York: Hyperion, 2005.

Keverne, Eric B., Nicholas D. Martensz, and Bernadette Tuite. "Beta-Endorphin Concentrations in Cerebrospinal Fluid of Monkeys Are Influenced by Grooming Relationships," *Psychoneuroendocrinology* 14, no. 1–2 (1989): 155–161.

Lipton, Bruce H., and Steve Bhaerman. *Spontaneous Evolution: Our Positive Future (and a Way to Get There From Here)*. Carlsbad, CA: Hay House, 2009.

Manne, Joy. *Conscious Breathing: How Shamanic Breathwork Can Transform Your Life*. Berkeley, CA: North Atlantic Books, 2004.

McGilchrist, Iain. *The Master and His Emissary: The Divided Brain and the Making of the Western World*. New Haven, CT: Yale University Press, 2009.

Montagu, Ashley. *Touching: The Human Significance of the Skin*. New York: Perennial Library, 1986.

Nelson, Charles A., Nathan A. Fox, and Charles H. Zeanah. *Romania's Abandoned Children: Deprivation, Brain Development, and the Struggle for Recovery*. Cambridge, MA: Harvard University Press, 2014.

Nolan, Dan, and Chris Amico. Solitary by the Numbers. *Frontline*. April 18, 2017. https://www.pbs.org/wgbh/frontline/article/solitary-by-the-numbers.

Pinker, Steven. *The Better Angels of Our Nature: Why Violence Has Declined*. New York: Penguin, 2011.

Pinker, Steven. *The Blank Slate: The Modern Denial of Human Nature*. New York: Penguin, 2002.

Pinker, Steven. *How the Mind Works*. New York: W. W. Norton, 1997.

Renfrew, Colin. *Prehistory: The Making of the Human Mind*. New York: Modern Library, 2008.

Rosen, Steven A., Arkady B. Savinetsky, Yosef Plakht, Nina Kisseleva, Bulat F. Khassanov, Andrey M. Pereladov, and Mordecai Haiman. "Dung in the Desert: Preliminary Results of the Negev Holocene Ecology Project," *Current Anthropology* 46, no. 2 (2005): 317–327.

Shlain, Leonard. *The Alphabet versus the Goddess: The Conflict between Word and Image*. New York: Penguin, 1998.

Shlain, Leonard. *Sex, Time, and Power: How Women's Sexuality Shaped Human Evolution.* New York: Penguin, 2004.

Skoyles, John, and Dorion Sagan. *Up from Dragons: The Evolution of Human Intelligence.* New York: McGraw-Hill, 2002.

Trefil, James. *Are We Unique? A Scientist Explores the Unparalleled Intelligence of the Human Mind.* New York: John Wiley & Sons, 1997.

Webster's New World College Dictionary. 4th ed. Cleveland, OH: Wiley, 2010.

Wilber, Ken. *Up from Eden: A Transpersonal View of Human Evolution.* Boulder, CO: Shambhala, 1981.

Young, Richard W. "Evolution of the Human Hand: The Role of Throwing and Clubbing," *Journal of Anatomy* 202, no. 1 (2003): 165–174.

Zajonc, Arthur. *Catching the Light: The Entwined History of Light and Mind.* New York: Oxford University Press, 1993.

CPSIA information can be obtained
at www.ICGtesting.com
Printed in the USA
LVHW092306260819
629045LV00001B/125/P

9 781982 220655